Style for all Seasons

DAVID & ELIZABETH EMANUEL
STYLE
FOR ALL SEASONS

PAVILION
MICHAEL JOSEPH

Photographs appear by kind permission of the following; photographers are given in brackets; an asterisk indicates the copyright holder is Pavilion Books: Walter Annenberg Collection 38 (top) Renoir: *Daughters of Catulle Mendes at Piano*; (Michel Arnaud) 83; (Clive Arrowsmith) 86, 87; Blackie Publishing Group: Flower Fairies by Cecily Mary Barker 37; Camera Press: (Lord Snowdon) 39, 46, 93, (Norman Parkinson) 112, (Cecil Beaton) 51, (Patrick Lichfield) 76/77, (John Bishop) 137, (Lionel Cherrault) 142; Chancery Lane Films Ltd 58, 59; Cliché Musées Nationaux Paris 67 Vigée-Lebrun: *Marie Antoinette à la Rose*; Colour Library International 73; Columbia Pictures (top – Bernard Prim—costume designer Anthony Powell) 57; Compiègne/Château, Photographie Giraudon 68 (top left) Winterhalter: *L'Impératrice Eugénie et ses dames d'honneur*; Condé Nast Publications Ltd: (Alex Chatelain) 2/3, 44, 117, (Alan Randall) 34, (Lord Snowdon) 41 (top), 70 (top), (Terence Donovan) 41 (bottom), (Anthony Crickmay) 69, 78, (François Lamy) 88; Daily Telegraph Colour Library 75 (top); (David Emanuel) 36; (Milton Greene) 154 (top); (David Grey) 45, 113; GTO Films 57 (centre – costume designer Judy Dorsman); John Heathcoat & Co Ltd (Anthony Crickmay) 42; Illustrated London News Picture Library 74 (top right); Innoxa (Stefano Massimo) 128, 129; (Neil Kirk) 33 (right); Kobal Collection 40 (top right), 52, 68 (bottom), 98 (right), 150; Lazzarini Collection 43 (bottom), 112 (top); (Patrick Lichfield) 30*, 31*, 64*, 65*, 106*, 107*, 134*, 135*; London Express News & Feature Services 75 (bottom), (John Adriaan) 85 and 157; London Newspaper Services Ltd (Peter Abbey) 74 (top left); The Mansell Collection 32 (top left), 121, 124; (Stefano Massimo) 82, 92, 119; The Metropolitan Museum of Art 38 (bottom) Renoir: *Madame Charpentier*; (Tim Motion) 10*, 12–21*, 23*; (David Montgomery) 24*, 54*, 80*, 98* (left), 138*, 143* (centre and bottom), 155*; (Chris Moyse) 25, Museum of London 43 (top); National Gallery of Art, Washington 40 Renoir: *The Dancer* (Widener Collection), 70 (bottom) Renoir: *Madame Monet and her son* (Ailsa Mellon Bruce Collection); National Magazine Company (Alberto dell'Orto) 139, 140/141, (Clive Arrowsmith) 152, 153; (Terry O'Neill) 159*; (Norman Parkinson) 94/95, 96/97, 99, 100*, 101*; (Robert Pascall) 79; Photographers International (Jayne Fincher) 84; Rex Features 158; (Charles Settrington) 28/29*, 62/63*, 104/105*, 132/133*; Sothebys Belgravia (Cecil Beaton) 50 (bottom), and 143 (top) courtesy Condé Nast Publications Inc; (John Swannell) 8, 48, 49, 108, 109, 122/123*, 126/127*, 144*, 145*, 146*, 147*, 148*, 149*; Tate Gallery 50 (top) Sir John Everett Millais: *Ophelia* 1852; (Mario Testino) 55, 56, 57 (bottom), 89, 90, 91; Victoria & Albert Museum, Theatre Museum 110; Wallace Collection 68 (top right); (Richard Young) 81.

Grateful acknowledgement is also made to the following for their assistance: make-up: Barbara Daly: 64, 65, 100, 101, 106, 107, 122, 123, 126, 127, 144–149, 159, and Glauca Rossi: 30, 31, 134, 135; hairdressing: John Frieda: 30, 31, 64, 65, 106, 107, 122/123, 126/127, 134, 135, 144–149, 159, and David Andrews: 100, 101; jewellery: Garrard: 64, 65, 106, 107, 134, 135, 144–149, 159, and Adrien Mann: 122/123, 126/127; silk flowers: Nimmos 64, 65, and Novelty Imports: 100, 101; bench loaned by Garden Crafts: 100, 101; tapestries loaned by Vigo-Sternberg Galleries: 122/123, 126/127; fur by Maxwell Croft: 134, 135; lacquered pillar loaned by Lady Sally Settrington: 134, 135; shoes by Ivory of Bond Street and Knightsbridge: 144–149.

First published in Great Britain in 1983 by
Pavilion Books Limited
196 Shaftesbury Avenue, London WC2H 8JL
in association with Michael Joseph Limited
44 Bedford Square, London WC1B 3DU

Copyright © 1983 Emanuel Designs Limited
Designed by Lawrence Edwards

All rights reserved. No part of this publication may be reproduced, stored in a retrieval system, or transmitted, in any form or by any means, electronic, mechanical, photocopying, recording or otherwise, without the prior permission of the copyright owner.

Emanuel, David
   Style for all seasons.
   1. Emanuel, David 2. Emanuel, Elizabeth 3. Costume design—Pictorial works
   I. Title II. Emanuel, Elizabeth
746.9′2 TT505.E/

ISBN 0—907516—13—0

Printed and bound in Italy by New Interlitho

Introduction

This is not our autobiography. How could it be—we've only just started out on our careers. We are not yet in our thirties, and with only five years in the fashion business behind us, we realise there is still a long way to go; we certainly do not consider that this book is our last word.

What it is about is the way we are inspired by the past and the present, and how we turn these inspirations into unashamedly romantic clothes. We have a great deal of fun finding new sources of inspiration and we love creating clothes which have a certain romantic and exhibitionistic quality about them, for women of every age and type.

To be any good at all at their profession, fashion designers must be aware that they live and work in a world that is preoccupied with change and development. Times and fashions change and the moods and desires of women change with them, sometimes even in advance of fashion. We've changed in the five years since we left art school and we want to continue to develop new moods and new ideas in the future, in our own particular style, just as we have done in the past.

In this book we have tried to give an idea of the sources of our inspiration, both contemporary and historical, and to show how these ideas are translated into our work to create a particular style for today, capable of being worn at any age, and ultimately, for all seasons.

Although it is often said that being asked to design the royal wedding dress made us an overnight success story, we like to think that we spent five years working hard to define and refine the Emanuel 'effect' and that when we were, totally unexpectedly, asked to design that most romantic of all dresses, we were ready for the once-in-a-lifetime opportunity and challenge.

One of the questions we are often asked is: 'What do you feel makes your clothes special . . . different?' For it is true to say that many people do recognise our designs when they see them, even though we do not put our initials on them. We hope this is because the Emanuel effect is distinctive. We are committed to designing clothes of a very romantic nature that are somewhat larger than life when viewed from a distance. When you look closely however, the positive shapes we design have something else to offer, as all sorts of nuances and subtleties are revealed. A flower on the shoulder grows from a hand-sequinned leaf; on close inspection a distant glitter of sequins crystallises into tiny flowers, hand-appliquéd on lace. This intentional double-take effect is the basis of our style, and our lives as designers have been spent striving to perfect and develop it into new images. How we achieve this look, what inspires us and our ideas of how one can project oneself in romantic clothes are all themes we shall consider in these pages.

Our ambition is always that each collection and every dress we design will be in some way an improvement on the one before, and we work extremely hard to produce new ideas which retain the Emanuel effect. This effect is of considerable importance to us, because unlike other designers who have symbols to identify their clothes, all we have is a love of romance, colour and delicate detail—and, we hope, a touch of magic too.

While we are in the process of writing this book and defining our inspirations, we are also working on our next big collection and naturally we are extremely enthusiastic about it. But six months after it has been shown to our clients and to the press we know that we will look back at the ideas and go through all of them with a new and more critical eye. We can never sit back and say: 'Well, that's over and done with'—and that is why we find it so rewarding working together as a husband and wife team, since there is always someone to bounce ideas off, to offer criticism and of course to be enthusiastic!

Although this book is by no means an autobiography, it is certainly all about our past, present and future ideas on design. We are not writers, we are designers and therefore draw much of our inspiration from photographs, paintings, films and illustrations. As designers, our vocabulary is a visual one, so whenever possible, we have used illustrations to convey our ideas.

We believe that every woman has the potential to be

stylish in her own way, whether she is eight or eighty, and in the past five years, we have dressed women of every age from Spring to Winter to prove it. We have never dictated or imposed our style on any of our clients, but we have always been ready to make suggestions and advise them on how best to express the individuality they were born with.

There isn't a title 'style designer' but there might well be, for style is not just different from fashion—it is almost its opposite. We are far more interested in developing individual style in people than in making them follow the dictates of group fashion. Almost by definition fashion does not last, but style does and it is consistent. Fashion is change for change's sake, and it is all about looking exactly the same as a great many other people. True style is concerned with the art of looking uniquely and unforgettably individual.

In creating this book on style, we hope to encourage a far wider audience than we could ever manage to design for personally to view style in this way. For we find it more of a challenge and a reward seeing real people, with real-life, less-than-perfect figures, wearing our clothes and looking extraordinary in them, than dressing the easier perfection of fashion models. Everything we do is aimed at making women look better than their previous best, in their and our own special way.

We have developed this specialised attitude to dressing during the five years we have been working as designers because we are in constant contact with all sorts of different clients, and have always endeavoured to discuss our ideas with them. We have become increasingly aware of the personality of the individual as a crucial part of the process of creating a new dress, and by encouraging our clients' awareness and confidence we also bring out their essential (if somewhat latent) style.

One of the constant problems we face however, is that unless a client is old enough to remember the early fifties (the last time romantic exhibitionist dresses were worn) she has probably never imagined herself looking marvellous in romantically extravagant designs. We are constantly telling our clients that although bouffant skirts may look difficult to wear we have in fact made it very easy. Some of the little soft elasticated dresses are just wisps of chiffon over separate tulle petticoats. The strapless ones are all boned very carefully so that as well as staying up (essential of course) they are undemanding to wear because their fit is both comfortable and exact.

Quite often, having seen pictures of our romantic effects in magazines, clients tell us when they first come into our salon that they couldn't possibly wear one of our bouffant dresses, as they are too extravagant or too large. But if we feel that a dress with a very full skirt could set off their personality and style, we try to persuade them to try one on and more often than not find they love the way they look.

All the pictures in this book have been chosen because they inspired us, and we hope they may influence you into developing your own notions about what will suit you and what will not. We have divided them into Spring, Summer, Autumn and Winter—the four seasons of style and also the four seasons of womanhood. You will find that you fit into one of these seasons, and may find that one of these styles is right for you. Adapt it to take into account your own taste, your figure type and the demands of the life you lead. If you do it your way, you will look wonderful and unique. We hope the ideas we put forward in this book will help you to determine your own personal approach to dressing. In showing you the sources of inspiration from which we have always drawn our Emanuel style, we hope that we inspire you too.

David Emanuel

&

Elizabeth Emanuel

We would like to extend our gratitude to all those who have contributed to this book—in particular a 'special' thank-you to the following:

HRH The Duchess of Kent for graciously sitting for her portrait.

All the personalities for allowing us to use their pictures, and the following for sitting for the book: Lysette Anthony, Marina Berni, Claire Bloom, Bryony Brind, Faye Dunaway, Wayne Eagling, Jane Seymour and Sophie Ward.

Colin Webb of Pavilion Books; Meredith Etherington-Smith; and David Armstrong of Garrards.

The Emanuel Ladies—Nina, Rose, Sara, Ines, and our assistant Allison, for turning our inspirations and fantasies into real clothes.

And a very special thank-you to Caroline Slocock for her unfaltering patience in checking and re-checking everything, and for her continued endless enthusiasm.

We would also like to thank the following for the very important part they have played in the preparation of this book: Patrick Lichfield, Stefano Massimo, Norman Parkinson, Charles Settrington, John Swannell and Mario Testino; Barbara Daly and Glauca Rossi; John Frieda; Lawrence Edwards; and Judy Dauncey.

To Oliver and Eloise

*our parents
and all our loyal clients...*

Style for all Seasons

Our very first inspiration in terms of developing our larger than life romantic look came when we were both at the Royal College of Art, studying for our M.A. Degrees. We had been at Harrow School of Art together, married at the end of our three years there and gone to the Royal College as the first married students ever to take the M.A. fashion course. Like so many students, we were both struggling to create our own quite distinct handwriting rather than producing designs which were influenced by the giants of the profession: designers like Valentino and Yves St Laurent. We admire both of them, but for our final diploma fashion show we wanted to create something—some mood—which was ours rather than derived from someone else.

Working in the Victoria & Albert Museum library one day, we chanced upon some books on Diaghilev's Ballets Russes and suddenly everything fell into place. The magnified quality of designs from artists such as Bakst, Gontcharova and Erté suited our feeling for more fantasy in design and more romance in effect, and became an inspiration that is still important to us years later.

That is not to say we live in the past. Fashion never comes back the way it left and nor does style. It returns, but in a new and different form, seen through fresh eyes. The woman dressed by Poiret—another designer who has influenced us—is not the same woman that might wear the gold lamé and monkey fur Poiret-inspired opera coat (see it on page 112 worn by Bianca Jagger) sixty years later. She thinks differently from her grandmother; her shape, hair and make-up are all different—and so, more importantly, is her entire way of life. She would look strange in an original Poiret, but re-interpreted in contemporary terms, she looks modern and magnificent.

Our final diploma show was inspired by the ballet, but the end result was our own. We felt we had at last established our handwriting. We were very lucky to have done so at that particular time, for in 1977, the world seemed to be ready to dress up again, and reaction to this all-white romantic collection was very encouraging to two extremely nervous fashion students starting up a business direct from college. Since then, we have developed this look in many different areas. Our sources of ideas and inspiration seem to grow wider and wider as we discover more about the past and understand more about the present, through books, through looking at old fabrics, from our clients' suggestions and from reactions to our work.

Films and television are more and more important in influencing the way people perceive themselves and the way they develop their style. We have always kept a few key images in mind when designing certain clothes—Greta Garbo, dressed, as shown on page 52, in white muslin with a leghorn hat by the brilliant Hollywood designer Adrian for *Camille*, or Vivien Leigh as the young Scarlett O'Hara in *Gone with the Wind* sitting on the porch in yards of organza (shown on the same page.)

Recently we have been given the opportunity of being involved in costume design ourselves, which has proved to be a new and fascinating experience. *Invitation to the Wedding* is the first time we have dressed someone for film, and we created the complete wardrobe for the star, Susan Brooks, ranging from jeans to the wedding dress itself. Ballet and pantomime are two of the performing arts which have inspired us in the past, and now we find ourselves being requested to develop designs for contemporary productions. Some of our ideas for the ballet are shown on pages 108–111, and our pantomime designs for *Cinderella* on pages 156–157.

Although fashion never comes back in exactly the same way, certain designers from the past seem to have relevance to what we are doing today: Poiret, for his scintillating oriental ideas; Schiaparelli's dramatic silhouettes and brilliant decorative detailing, notably in her 'Circus' collection for which she created beaded mosaics of circuses, individually sewn onto tight-fitting jackets; Callot Soeurs, who made dresses as fine as dragon-fly wings in tissues and silk chiffons to dress the famous dancer Florence Walton; and of course, Erté.

When we say inspiration, we really do mean inspiration, not repetitive variations. We may look at a

painting or drawing and find just one tiny detail that makes us pause for thought and sets us thinking along certain lines; from these a whole series of ideas spring which may seem quite unrelated to their original source. All these marvellous images fuel our creativity and eventually emerge in the form of a new collection.

In fact paintings are probably our most important source of inspiration: Renaissance portraits of haughty beauties dressed in rich collages of figured velvets and brocades, Pre-Raphaelite paintings of willowy women with garlands of flowers tangled in their flowing hair and Picasso's portraits of Sylvia, with her youthful angularity. We find a good deal to admire in the jig-saw patterns and soft dreamlike colours used by Gustav Klimt and are greatly influenced by the beauty of the paintings of Botticelli.

How do we start to create our collections? In a sense the process is already underway every time we open a book about Pre-Raphaelite painting; every time we go to costume sales at Phillips or Christies; every time we buy another piece of antique lace. But sooner or later all these influences must actually appear in dress form and that is when we close the doors of our salon and workrooms and get down to some really hard work.

This always starts with sketches. These are literally fleeting thoughts put down quickly on paper. They establish the mood and the flavour of the collection. At this stage they are very rough, but they are the first (and often most difficult) step towards the final show. We may sketch out literally hundreds of these little ideas before we start working on them in earnest, putting in suggestions for details, altering and revising the shapes, and correcting the proportions. Many ideas never make it beyond the drawing board, whereas others grow and grow, take on a life of their own and become important sections of the collection.

At about the same time, we will be looking at fabrics. We search out new fabrics all the time, and some of those that we will have found during the course of the year will themselves prove to be inspirational. In other cases, we know exactly what we are looking for, and then have to deliberately search the fabric out. It is not a question of simply going to a fabric trade fair and picking out whatever is currently available. In our quest for unusual or unique fabrics, we may have to commission mills as far away as India. Sometimes we will discover a marvellous material quite by accident, which is even more exciting for us. Our finely pleated silks, hand-dyed to create ever-changing harmonies of colour, for example, led to a whole series of ideas based on Botticelli's glorious painting of girls in Spring, *Primavera*. Of course we know the painting well—is there an art student who doesn't? But seeing the fabric acted as a catalyst for a series of designs influenced by the mood of the painting.

Sometimes we will take the simplest of fabrics and hand-embroider it to create a visual deception. It looks simple at first glance but we like our designs to become more intriguing the closer you look at them, which is why we hand-embroider fine white cotton lawn with art-nouveau and Victorian broderie anglaise motifs, inspired by some of the beautiful work on nineteenth century petticoats and camisoles.

At other times, a painting itself will strike a chord. The carefree beauty of Fragonard's *The Swing* suggested many subsequent ideas for trimming dresses with tiny white bows and garlanding shoulders with flowers. Finding new stimuli is a constant process and probably the most exciting part of creating a collection.

Ideas, however, are not enough. They have to work, which is why every dress we design is actually made and fitted on a living model, just as we make our clients' dresses on them, rather than on a dressmaker's dummy. There is not anything unusual in this; most French couturiers work this way, and we believe it is extremely important as the living body is such an integral factor in our designs. Every dress in our collection is tried on again and again. We seem to spend endless time on the floor trimming tulle petticoats or pinning hems, but all this attention to detail is worth it at the end of the day as we think this is partly what makes an Emanuel dress special.

Once we have the basic structure of the dress right, we then add the decoration, which must always accentuate yet never impose on the shape and fabric. Some dresses need flowers on the shoulder or some such bold detailing. Other dresses need delicate filigree embroidery, or an overlay of mother-of-pearl sequins. Sometimes our tulle petticoats are embroidered too, so that they show through the gauzy dress, to give a subtle, half-seen effect, mysterious and delicate.

We make nearly all of our embroidery and decorations in our workrooms. We do collect silk flowers, however, wherever we find them. Some are made for us, but we really treasure the wonderfully muted colours of the antique examples we come across from time to time. We often embroider net with mother-of-pearl sequins, and all this is done by hand. We also design little bags (to pin at the waist), gloves, wreaths of flowers—and all these small details add up to the Emanuel style.

Unlike most fashion designers who show a Spring/Summer collection and an Autumn/Winter collection, we do only one major show each year, so this collection spans the four seasons—from the fresh youthful dresses we design for teenagers to the more glamorous sophisticated creations worn at really grand occasions by more mature women.

Every season has its own rules and its own demands, so we plan our show in groups, all of which evolve from the mood of that particular collection, but which are interpreted in different ways and different fabrics, according to the season. Velvet is not usually associated with Spring, just as white cotton lawn is not often thought of for Winter. But sometimes, just to be paradoxical, we might incorporate white velvet in a dress for Spring, or team opaque black tights with white cotton lawn dresses—we enjoy using unlikely combinations of fabrics to create unusual effects.

Spring however is mostly based on natural meadow colours. We try to achieve a simple, uncontrived look that Botticelli expressed so well when he painted Simonetta Vespucci in the fifteenth century.

Another inspiration for Spring is the pretty white late-Victorian lingerie that we find in costume and lace sales. Two recent films have also started us working in this direction, *Tess* and *Picnic at Hanging Rock*—the latter about muslin-clad and be-ribboned Victorian schoolgirls in the Australian outback.

We often use lace over net for children's dresses in our collection, but we always choose a very delicate pattern on a small scale, like Brussels or Mechlin, which are both really net with tiny flowers and leaves as the thread motifs. The bolder patterns, such as the fern-like Valenciennes or the scrolled motifs of Point de Venise, we save for the more dramatic wedding dresses or ball-gowns.

Children's clothes of the past are a valid inspiration for children's clothes of the present, which we love designing. Here, we have found that scale is very important. Nothing must be overdone or exaggerated; everything must be proportionately small and delicately detailed. The smaller the child the finer the detailing. By all means embroider a little pearl or two on the bodice of a party frock or bridesmaid's dress, but let them be the tiniest seed pearls. Flame-proof nylon net in many gauzy layers can also look pretty for little children; we like to scatter tiny little silk rosebuds on each layer so that it shows through as a misty effect. This can be particularly effective for small bridesmaids. Another look we like is that achieved by trimming each layer of net with narrow lace edging, letting it peep out layer by layer. We also use minute silk flowers to scatter over an elasticated neckline.

The construction of these dressed-up clothes for children need not be complicated. We have always liked to elasticise delicate fabrics, as they become so easy to pull on and off and you can hide the line of elastic at the waist, as we do, with a pretty satin or moiré sash. Elasticated necklines are practical for small children too, because the child's head is usually quite big in proportion to the rest of the body. It is much easier to slip the dress over the head rather than struggle with a wriggling and irritated child while trying to do up millions of buttons! Dressing small

children can be such fun, and there is nothing to equal the enchantment of a tiny child in a fairylike dress setting off as a bridesmaid or going to her first party.

The ground rules for the first steps in style are to make sure you keep everything small, fresh, neat and light. And what goes with this style in embryo? Flat pink or white satin or leather ballet pumps, worn with white cotton socks or tights. For a very special event perhaps you might, as we do, make a wreath of tiny silk flowers, which is very easy. You can buy the flowers on wired stalks and just twine the stems together into a little crown that should sit firmly but not uncomfortably on the child's head. Ravishing!

Spring is also associated with teenagers, and we have a great deal of fun dressing this age group. They are so often unconventional in their approach to dressing. They always know exactly how they want to wear something and we find that, invariably, their view does not follow the original design.

Teenagers are sometimes casual in the way they will treat their clothes but this attitude can be very stimulating when it comes to designing for them. They might, for example, take one of our silk chiffon dresses and hitch it up over their knees, showing a white Victorian petticoat underneath; or they might wear a white lawn mini-dress over bleached and tattered jeans. We remember one girl who appeared in English *Vogue* not long ago who wore our ballgowns with a spiky punk hairdo and a diamond tiara. A lot of people might have been horrified at this combination of crinoline, tiara, punk hair and very little make-up, but we thought it was great fun because it somehow captured exactly the jaunty teenage spirit and their casual scorn of convention.

There is a vast choice of fabrics and effects for teenagers and as long as the finished idea isn't too overpowering or grand, they look good in just about everything. We like to see them in very constructed stiff silk taffetas with narrow lace edging, but worn about three inches above the ankle with flat shoes, as the silhouette of a full-length dress would be a little too imposing for them.

Teenagers also look very fresh and pretty in white or pastel organdie or organza trimmed with narrow ribbon or lace, and of course they look marvellously fresh in floating chiffons simply elasticated at neck and waist. We like to hand-tint these chiffons so that they only give a hint of colour.

One of the important things about the clothes we make for our clients, whatever their age, is that our designs are adaptable for a variety of occasions. We believe that the soft romantic effects we create can be worn in many different ways. You could, for instance, wear a lightly elasticated chiffon dress, which is really nothing more than a gathered tunic, by itself, or over one of our net petticoats. By itself the dress would be reminiscent of Botticelli's *Primavera*, but with the addition of the petticoat it becomes a Scarlett O'Hara dress. Versatile, and two looks for one.

We keep these young clothes very simple in terms of construction. A strapless cotton voile dress can be shirred to keep it up, rather like a fifties bathing suit, and thus will not need boning. As with dresses for little girls, we elasticate waists and necklines so that a deep elasticated and frilled 'V' can simply be pulled off the shoulder for a totally different effect, and a waistline can be pulled down or up to alter the shape of the dress.

If teenage clients insist on glitter we always try to keep the finished effect light and semi-transparent. Iridescent mother-of-pearl sequins sprinkled here and there are far more effective in maintaining a young fresh look than solid gold sequins could ever be.

When we're developing an idea into a series of dresses we tend to have an actual person in mind. Since we started as designers there has always been someone who has influenced the way we look at and design clothes at a particular moment. Our cover girl, eighteen-year-old Sophie Ward, has been a great inspiration when we've been thinking about fresh young clothes. She has a marvellous simplicity and freshness whatever she wears. She's young, pretty, with a natural delicacy—the perfect spirit of Spring.

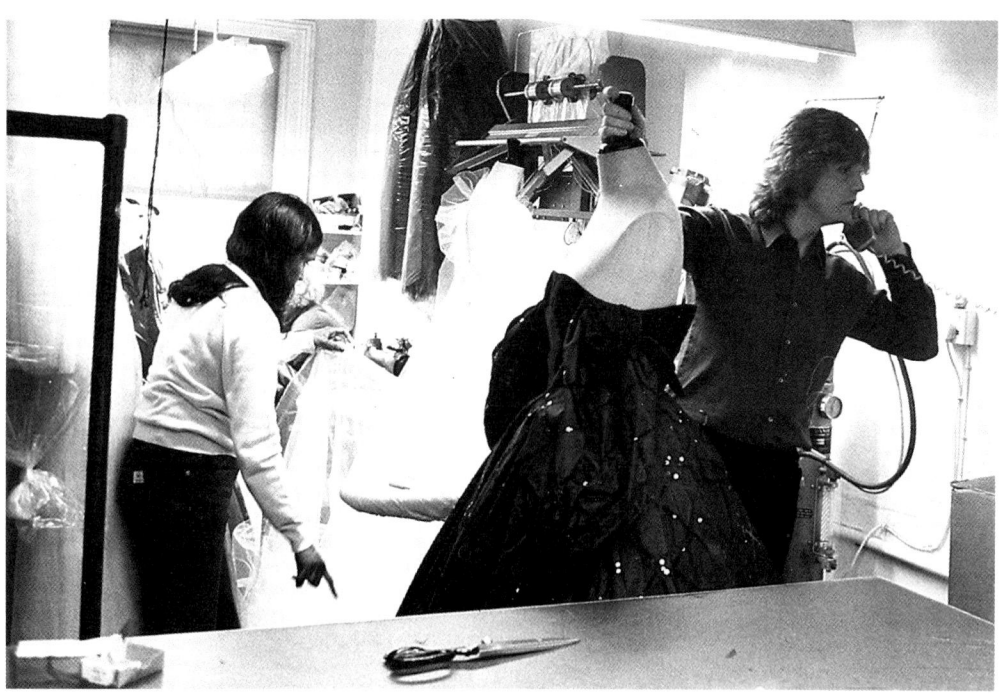

Summer, as a style, should be more sophisticated. It is for the woman who has grown up, who naturally wants to establish a more worldy ambience than that of a teenager. Instead of the fluttering, almost transparent dresses for Spring, our summer style has always evolved from the idea of a more studied effect and is based around many layers of airy fabric which build up into a more definite shape. Summer designs are much more controlled than our filmy spring dresses. They have more shape built into them, making the most of the person who is going to wear them. Boned and sculptured bodices, for instance, make the figure look fantastic and that is why so many of our summer ballgowns are based on the combination of strict, structured bodices, bared shoulders and very full layer-upon-layer skirts. It is a look inspired by Degas and Renoir, whose superbly blooming women are dressed in billowing clouds of fabric. Summer is flowers in full bloom, at their peak of heavy scentedness and beauty, and our dresses reflect that inspiration.

In the Summer we are most frequently asked for ballgowns and wedding dresses. For both occasions, although the demands on the dresses are different, we are influenced by the rococo look of Marie Antoinette as she was so frequently painted by Madame Vigée-Lebrun, or the modern re-creation of this eighteenth century style, personified by Marisa Berenson in Stanley Kubrick's film *Barry Lyndon*. The other great heroine of Summer is the Empress Eugénie as painted by Winterhalter in the mid-nineteenth century. We love the splendidly decorative ballgowns in delicate colours, the clouds of net and tulle, the garlands of flowers.

But apart from such inspirations from the past, fabrics are a good starting point in themselves. For instance we may look at a spotted net and a design will suggest itself. We almost seem to be able to see the finished dress in front of us before we have even sketched the idea. For Summer we have always used a huge variety of fabrics—some of them rather unexpected ones. There is net of course, spotted voiles, cotton voile, broderie anglaise, organzas, hand-tinted chiffons and hand-tinted antique lace and silk tulle. We even use solid translucent sequins to create a glassy effect. We create effects on top of the existing fabric too: cobwebs of mother-of-pearl sequins and seed pearls, which are scattered at random or embroidered onto the pattern in the cloth.

We also use a great many flowers to add delicacy and delight to our summer ballgowns and wedding dresses. Big full-blown silk roses, delicate little flowers like lily of the valley, tiny starry ones like miniature roses and celandines. And the deep glossy green of leaves is a wonderful contrast to pure white net.

We find it interesting to contrast textures by, for instance, putting antique lace over silk tulle or over silk satin. Quite often, taking our inspiration from the magnificent fabrics of the turn of the century and the twenties, we embroider over the motifs on the lace with gold or mother-of-pearl sequins—even perhaps with knots and ribbon bows

But of all the summer dresses we design for our clients, by far the most challenging commission is to be asked to design their wedding dress. What is so wonderful about this is that there really are very few practical aspects to a wedding dress. It can be pure fantasy, bearing no relationship to the demands of everyday life. The whims of fashion and future wearability are of little or no consideration to most girls who are about to be married. If our clients are any example, they know it is one of the few times in their lives when the only demand they are going to make on the dress is that it should simply make them look more beautiful than they have ever looked before. And we of course are willing accomplices.

In spite of the apparent simplicity of designing a wedding dress, weddings can be extremely complicated occasions for us to get absolutely right, though less so if we are asked to dress the bridesmaids and pageboys as well, as then we can co-ordinate all the detail. The first question we always ask when a bride comes in to see us is 'when'—this may sound somewhat irrelevant (apart from giving us an idea of how long we have to make the dress) but it isn't. This is because when we are planning the look

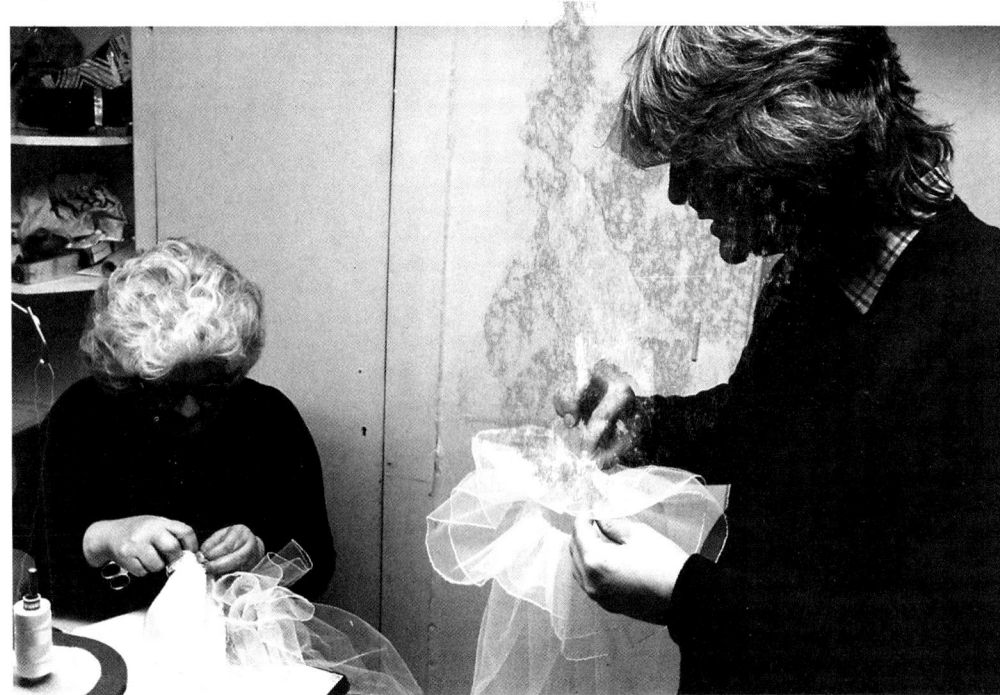

of a wedding, we take into account what sort of atmosphere there is likely to be on the wedding day; the light, the time of day, the time of year, the flowers that will be available—all these elements influence our thinking. There is no point, after all, in designing a wedding dress for September based on flowers that are only available in June—and for us flowers play an important part in our approach to wedding dress design.

And then we ask 'where'. A dress for a country church wedding will obviously be planned on a very different scale to one designed to be worn in a cathedral, chapel or registry office. We like to have a pretty accurate idea of the size of the church, how many people will be at the wedding, and what sort of reception there is going to be afterwards, because all these factors will influence certain practical aspects of the design of the dress. For a small church, for instance, a very long train would look too bulky and out of scale with the size of the wedding. For a large church or cathedral—St Paul's for example—a lengthy train such as the one we designed for Lady Diana is vital if the bride is to be seen at her best as she walks down a long aisle.

We designed a wedding dress that glittered with mother-of-pearl sequins for the marriage of Candia Wallop, because St Martin's-in-the-Field, where she married, was very dark, and we felt that it would achieve a most telling effect if the bride's dress shone luminously in the gloom.

As the bride herself has to be the centre of the picture we try to find out whether she has an ideal in mind, for of course we want to design the dress of her dreams if we possibly can. Sometimes, however, it is difficult to sort out just what a bride wants. At other times, her 'dream' could well turn out to be a nightmare, and we then have to bring a great deal of tact into play. We did have one client who was absolutely determined that her wedding dress should be transparent, and we had some difficulty persuading her that she must wear something underneath the layers of tulle she had set her heart on.

Ideally, we like to design and plan every aspect of the wedding 'picture'. This means not only designing the bride's dress and bouquet but also planning her hair, her head-dress, make-up, jewellery, shoes and even tights. To complete the picture, we also like to design the bridesmaids' and pageboys' outfits and will even offer advice on the decorations for the church. This comprehensive approach is, we think, very important, because it is from the co-ordination of the myriad of seemingly tiny details that the perfection of the picture is achieved.

In our experience, one of the most frequent mistakes made by brides is to get the dress right, but the head-dress wrong. If, for example, you have a very full dress with a lot of detail then everything else should be very simple. Do not go mad with an over-elaborate head-dress and veiling; try to get the balance right, rather than consider each element in the final picture separately.

There are several basic rules to which we tend to adhere when designing a really grand wedding dress. One of them is to make the train detachable. There is nothing worse than going to a wedding and seeing the bride towing her train around, getting it crumpled and torn. Another rule, as we have mentioned, is 'long aisle, long train'. In creating an effect that is beautiful overall, the sight of a long train in a magnificent setting is quite unforgettable, as you can see on page 75.

Quite often people forget that the bridesmaids will be very much part of the picture too, and if the bride and her mother spend all their time thinking about the wedding dress the bridesmaids can sometimes become an afterthought, put into any old thing bought at the last moment. We always tell our clients that they should try and plan the bridesmaids' dresses to complement their wedding dress and by so doing make the whole impression harmonious. If, for instance, the bridesmaids are to be in white as well as the bride, we make sure the whites don't clash.

Whenever possible, we suggest the use of fresh flowers in the hair, rather than an artificial circlet. Most flowers will stay fresh if properly wired to last through the day. From the point of view of both look and fragrance flowers cannot be bettered. We do not often use formal, contrived

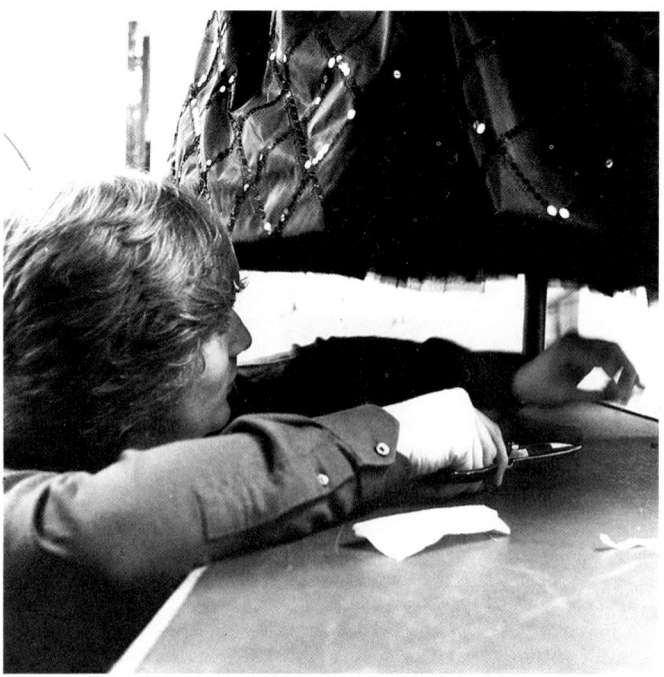

bouquets, apart from Victorian posies. A more natural, uncontrived look is so much prettier and softer, as if the flowers had just been picked from the garden.

Simple, natural looks are perfect for country weddings, particularly the classical June wedding. Try using trailing ivy and roses in full bloom. But avoid a very grand effect, for this could look wrong in the country. A country church wedding dress should obviously look much simpler and more spontaneous than a dress for a wedding in a cathedral or large town church.

The most thrilling commission we have ever received was to design Lady Diana Spencer's wedding dress for her marriage to HRH The Prince of Wales, and certainly one could never hope to be honoured with a more challenging commission than this—a dress which, at a conservative estimate, was to be seen by seven hundred million people!

When the engagement was announced we did not think for one minute that we had any chance of being given this extraordinary commission, but naturally, as every other British designer must have done, we dreamed.

When we learned that Lady Diana had chosen us and we were to have the enormous privilege of designing this most special of dresses, our lives suddenly became pandemonium. The press literally besieged us in our small salon just off Bond Street. They went through our waste-bins with the idea of finding clues in the form of scraps of fabric, or discarded sketches, so we had to keep everything relating to our work in an enormous safe we had installed. They peered through our windows from buildings opposite with telephoto lenses, so for three months we worked with all our blinds down and our workrooms and salon were constantly lit by electric light, even in the middle of the sunniest June day. Luckily, we managed to keep the secret by mentioning to everyone who asked us that we were actually making six dresses and that only we and Lady Diana knew which one she would finally wear. Of course this wasn't true! We laid a few other false trails too, such as throwing scraps of white silk away when we were actually making the one and only dress in ivory silk taffeta.

When we were asked to design the dress, we suspected it was because we were known for making very romantic and dramatic dresses, both essential requirements for the wedding of the century. Having paced out the aisle at St Paul's, we found that it took about three and a half minutes to walk from the main doors up to the altar rail, so a very long train was the first aspect of the design we decided upon. It did seem enormous though, when all twenty five feet of it was crammed in billows all over our small salon.

The Lullingstone Silk Farm, the only one in Britain, spun the silk thread and we commissioned Stephen Walters Limited to weave it into exceptionally heavy taffeta for us. They had never woven anything as dense before, but we wanted it to be so heavy that creases would fall out of it from its own weight. We spent days squashing up samples of the fabric in our hands and waiting to see whether the creases would fall out again. This quality of the material became an essential virtue when we realised how small was the space inside the state coach into which the dress would have to be confined. Another factor in our decision to design a very grand, full dress was that it gave us the opportunity to accomplish what we do best—our intricate, delicate handwork which is shown superbly in close-up. As the Princess was going to be seen by millions of people in close-up, as well as from afar, this was the one occasion when our 'double-take' effect of dramatic, bold shape and intricate, almost miniaturistic detailing could really come into its own, in life and on the television screen.

The design of the dress happened spontaneously and did not take very long because we felt that it had to be a dress of unique quality, that could not have been worn at any other time, or on any other occasion.

We realised that the detailed handwork would be so important as apart from anything else, it would make the dress extremely difficult to copy. It was very intricate and obviously we couldn't send it out to be embroidered and so Elizabeth and her mother embroidered the dress themselves, sitting up night after night, rather than allow it to leave our premises. It was kept in our maximum security safe, guarded by two security men.

The finished dress, especially sketched for this book by Elizabeth, is very dramatic but we like to think that the ultimate effect is paradoxically one of extravagant simplicity. The shape is very large but it is simple and defined, and the embroidery can only really be seen in close-up. We decided to sprinkle the beautiful lace and veil with tiny mother-of-pearl sequins so that the Princess would literally sparkle under all the lights in the Cathedral.

The final touch of detail was one we have not divulged until now. We sewed just one emblem onto the heart-shaped pot-pourri on the hanger—it was a tiny gold daffodil, representing Wales.

As you can see from our designs for the Royal Wedding, we were convinced that it was not enough to consider the bride by herself. In addition, we had to think how to frame her with bridesmaids, pages, flowers, bouquet—all these are just as important in creating the total picture.

The royal wedding day itself was an awesome occasion. So much work, thought, loving attention and concentration had gone into creating the dress. Months of trying to keep everything secret from people whose profession it is to find out. We dreamt, or had nightmares, that the dress would appear in sketch form before the final day but it never did, thanks to our loyal work-room staff and to all our security precautions.

When we saw Lady Diana, her bridesmaids and her pages walk up the aisle at St Paul's Cathedral, we felt all this effort and all the thought we had put into the most important wedding dress we would ever design had been rewarded a thousand-fold; and we know that the image of that moment will remain with us for ever.

Every bride that we dress presents a different challenge to us. Some choose to be married in a registry office rather than a cathedral and here we work to a different set of rules. Of course it would be wrong in such cases to provide the drama of a full dress, train and veil. Nevertheless, many registry office brides these days do not want to be deprived of the romance the occasion promises and then our advice is always to forget the veil and the train and settle for a really beautiful dress, possibly in a very pale tinted colour.

One registry office bride we really loved dressing was Susan Hampshire, for her wedding to the theatrical impresario Eddie Kulukundis. We had already made the wardrobe for her play *House Guest*, which included a dress with a gathered scoop neck, elasticated waist, sleeves to the elbow and a double circle skirt. She loved the shape and it worked very well for her on stage, so she decided to have it repeated as her wedding dress. She wanted it to be quite bright as she was getting married in the Autumn and feared that it might be a dull day, so we chose a white silk chiffon with a shocking pink pattern on it. We substituted a loose sash for the tailored belt she had worn on stage, and under the filminess of the patterned chiffon, we made a silk satin petticoat so that the dress frilled and swirled.

We think that a soft little dress like this is the perfect outfit for a romantic registry office wedding. It all depends on the bride's looks and taste—the best advice we can give is to keep to something that you know suits you. Soft pretty dresses are absolutely right for some people; for others a more tailored suit with perhaps a really extravagant hat and a pretty blouse would be better.

In preparing our collection, and trying to reflect the lives our clients lead with the appropriate designs for all seasons, we never forget holiday clothes. It is the other side of Summer and the get-away style demands quite a different sort of design language—bolder, brighter and simpler. After all, no one wants to iron yards of tulle on holiday. What is needed is not only simplicity but stunning effect as well.

The quality of light in the Mediterranean, for example, is quite different from that of the English countryside. It is obviously much harsher and stronger, so we design our holiday effects much more boldly and definitely in response. Our clothes for the English Summer are ethereal, in pale colours and with intricate detailing, but

our ideas for holiday clothes are completely different. We like to work in really vivid colours, to define the shape very sharply, and keep decorative detailing to a minimum—perhaps a stiff frill or a ruched neckline, as you can see in the photographs on pages 90 and 91.

We love the vibrant effect of raw silk dyed shocking-pink, deep turquoise, brilliant kingfisher blue or bright red. This is quite a stiff fabric and we like to cut it into sinuous body-hugging silhouettes, based on corset design, and we have carried this idea through into our collection of vividly coloured swimsuits. These are sexy, direct clothes, and should be worn with much harder, more defined make-up. Think of the hot nights of carnival in Rio, or the haughtiness of Spanish flamenco dancers!

There is another sort of holiday style we like and which we are always making for our clients, and that is the sophisticated but simple wrap-around dressing, indirectly inspired by that Coca Cola of the fashion world, the cotton-jersey T-shirt. We use cotton, fine wool and silk jersey to create billowing shapes that can simply be wrapped round the body in a casual almost scarf-like way. We might start with a huge simple shirt, worn over full elasticated pants, or an overtunic sashed round the waist with a jersey cardigan on top, and an optional skirt underneath. These stylish co-ordinating pieces (and there can be several interchangeable ones which go together) are the simplest and most practical way to dress for everyday summer.

Just like T-shirts they pull on easily, needing no complicated buttons or zips, and can be wrapped around in a way to suit the wearer. We like these co-ordinates in clear bright colours, or in pale honey beiges and white. We never use embroidery as the effect we aim for is an almost architectural starkness. The softness and drape of these clothes means that they can be knotted, wrapped and twisted into a really enormous variety of shapes. They can be worn casually or they can be worn dramatically, but they can also be packed into the smallest of suitcases for travelling. Useful and effective, they could not be more different from our romantic crinolines, but they reflect the very varied demands our clients make in terms of the stylish clothes they require, from ballgowns to the briefest of swimsuits.

Of course apart from our clients, the most important projection of our clothes to a wider audience is in the form of fashion photography. Right from the start, we have always been very involved in the process of transferring a dress to the printed page. Our first experience of fashion photography was with John Swannell, who took pictures of our RCA diploma show for *Ritz* magazine, and who has since photographed our designs on many occasions.

To create effects for photography demands just as much time and attention to detail as designing for the catwalk. Usually fashion magazines commission photographs using clothes they have seen in our collections but sometimes we make things especially for a particular feature. Last year, for instance, we made a red taffeta and black velvet Spanish-influenced dress for *Harper's & Queen* which they wished to use for the cover. Incredibly, it was made in just two and half days, but it worked visually because the effect was strikingly carried through to make-up and hair, as can be seen in the photographs on pages 139 and 140/1.

If we commission our own photographs, for instance, for advertising purposes, we always try to do the session with the same team because we work to similar standards, and it shows in the final result. We rarely design dresses for photographs, but they do seem to lend themselves to photographic treatment as they reflect such definite moods. We commissioned a number of photographs especially for this book from Patrick Lichfield, who photographed for us the spirits of Spring, Summer, Autumn and Winter—represented by Marina Berni, Jane Seymour, Bryony Brind and Claire Bloom. We planned every detail of each photograph, from the lacquered black wreath symbolising Winter, to the recreation of Botticelli's seashell for Spring. In some ways, getting the photographic session exactly right is very similar to creating a wedding effect. Every detail counts, and enables the photographer to capture the mood of the

picture exactly, in the same way that the bride can have the confidence that everything around her is helping to create a harmonious whole. We are relentless in our pursuit of the smallest bead if it will make what we consider to be all the difference!

Autumn is a glorious season for us because it is the season of parties, of theatricality and dressing up for dances where elaborate effects are perfectly in order.

We have always been inspired by the exuberance and projection of ballet costumes and over the last year or so the ballet itself has become a major inspiration to us. We go to the ballet a great deal and have even started to design ballet costumes. It is a medium which demands from us wild flights of fantasy—wilder indeed than anything one could wear in real life, and yet subtly this emphasis on the dramatic is influencing our annual collection too.

It's the contrast that fascinates us. From the front of the proscenium arch all is mystery and magic. Insubstantial figures seem to float effortlessly in mid-air. But we have also stood in the wings at Covent Garden and watched the ethereal ballerina float off-stage and suddenly slump to the floor gasping for breath. That apparent ease is suddenly transformed into aching muscles, sweat and nerves. It's a unique opportunity to see myth and reality at almost the same moment.

We also watch dancers exercising, warming themselves up at the barre in sweaters, leg warmers and tights. Layer upon layer is gradually peeled off as the dancers get warmer. As a practical demonstration of elegance under pressure, a dancer cannot be equalled and these heterogeneous exercising outfits put on for warmth and protection rather than for effect, nonetheless harmonise in all sorts of unexpected ways and encourage us to create new ways of dressing.

But the prime inspiration of the ballet concerns colour and mood. The vivid fancies of Bakst, the charming Victorian fairy costumes, and above all, the timeless beauty of Pavlova, continue to fascinate us and have all contributed to our development as designers. We love the Bilibin design for Pavlova as the Enchanted Bird Princess in a barbaric Russian costume lavishly encrusted with pearls and other stones which is shown on page 112.

We are also interested in the more oriental fantasies of the Ballets Russes which influenced Poiret to create some of his greatest efforts before the First World War. The materials he used were rich and strange, and the breadth of his imagination is extraordinary, even to the jaded contemporary eye. We think that as an inspiration for autumn ball dresses, this richly evocative mood can scarcely be equalled.

We have not only been inspired by ballet costumes, we have also learned a great deal about how to achieve both delicate and magical clothes that have to undergo very strenuous wear. Ballet dancers have a really tough time and so do their costumes. Visits to the theatre costume department of the Victoria & Albert Museum and the Royal Opera House have given us a valuable insight into such things as making bodices that hook up easily, and *stay* hooked. There is no room for a mistake in a ballet costume!

We've been working recently on designing costumes for two of the premiers danseurs of the Royal Ballet, Wayne Eagling and Bryony Brind. They create workshop ballets and we've designed the spider costumes for a ballet choreographed by Wayne Eagling entitled *Deadlier than the Male*. This is a real challenge to be imaginative, and to work on a scale which will give a definite effect from quite far away. It has meant re-thinking the way we make these clothes and the scale of our detailed handwork—innovations which have proved helpful when it comes to designing our own collection.

Other sources of inspiration for Autumn are the richly textured details of Renaissance and Pre-Raphaelite painters. Rich brocades, velvets, cloth of gold, bodices edged in fur, the use of cut velvet, and the wonderful flow and movement of these clothes have become a catalyst for new designs.

Deep, powerful colours in strange but harmonious combinations in paintings by artists such as Burne-Jones,

Rossetti and Millais are marvellous stimuli, setting our minds exploring down new paths. For if Spring and Summer are light and ethereal, Autumn, and indeed Winter, are luxurious and opulent with touches of magic in colour and in embroidery.

A visit to India some years ago was also very important to us. Apart from having the luck to discover that one can still obtain gold gauze of the type that Poiret always used, we also realised how many possible ways there were of using rich gold brocades, shot tissues, and very elaborate and brightly coloured embroidery.

We brought back many pieces of old fabrics that looked just like huge patchworks, which we used as the basis of our Indian collection. The tiny gold coins Indian women wear as bracelets were transformed into collar and cuff trimmings. The rich saffrons and purples, the brilliant crimsons and greens, and the wash of gold overall—so typically Indian—were used to create a collection of autumn clothes reflecting something of the gypsy dancer, something of the dressing-up box, and perhaps something of the glittering fantasy of Bakst or Poiret.

Of the four seasons, Autumn is when fantasy really comes into its own in our collection. Rich vibrant colours, fabrics encrusted with gold, brocade re-embroidered with sequins and pearls, elaborate decorative trimmings can all be brought into play, so that when a woman wearing one of these dresses arrives for that special occasion, she is the personification of the sumptuous glamour of the autumnal spirit.

Winter, on the other hand, we tend to treat in a different way—or rather in two different ways. First, we design extremely sophisticated dresses, often in black on black, or in deep rich colours such as peony-crimson. We concentrate on defined shape which is sometimes set off by the very controlled colour and details of elaborate embroidery. Often our winter designs are monochrome—black and white with detailing in the same colour. These are very subtle, sophisticated dresses.

We also design dresses for Winter which have warmth about them—in textures and warm colours which are for winter entertaining, in private, as opposed to the public impact of the monochrome dresses. We rarely show these dresses as they are made entirely on commission from our clients. Both sorts of design demand absolute polish and sophistication to carry them off and are therefore perfect for the mature woman who knows what suits her, and has disciplined her wardrobe to the simplest shapes, the most subtle of decorative effects.

Some of the costumes Adrian designed for Greta Garbo in *Queen Christina* are striking signposts to this style of dressing. They show the skilful use of warmly-textured fabrics such as velvet, combined with fur—trimming the hems or wrapped around the shoulders—to create marvellous Winter Queen effects.

In a sense, Winter is the opposite to Summer's obvious ethereal effect. Black lace not white, black velvet rather than white net. Black or white fur rather than garlands of roses. The seasons are poles apart in terms of materials and decoration, but for us they both lend themselves to the same double-take effect of a bold shape and intimate, delicate handwork. For example, we stitch black sequins onto black lace to give a frostily sparkling look. We trim black velvet with white fox to create a stunning monochrome effect of texture against texture.

Winter is dramatic in a very different way from Autumn. It is discipline as opposed to extravagance. Still opulent, it depends on a much stricter control of texture and colour than is seen for Autumn. Winter white, banded with fur; winter black, trimmed in black sequins. Scarlet and black for an old-fashioned Christmas look. The look must always be richly textured, and if we add embroidery it is in order to increase the visual depth of the fabric—black sequins on black satin, dulled gold sequins on gold brocade. We aim for an almost three dimensional tonal effect, rather than one of contrasts.

Winter designs have body and weight and are cut in very precise shapes. They are simple and crisp. Frills fan out stiffly, rather than ruffle—it's a much more architectural approach which we find suits the more formal aspect of winter dances or grand galas. Suiting the season too, this

rather stiff, sculptural approach comes into its own against the clarity of frosty skies and the harsher light of winter—a look that was practised to perfection by Balenciaga and the American designer Charles James, both past masters of the art of the structured ballgown. The era of these truly sophisticated ballgowns really started after the Second World War and continued through the fifties as exhibited by such virtuosi as Jacques Fath and Dior. But the youth revolution of the sixties put paid to this sort of designing by demanding much lighter, freer clothes. Judging by our clients' requests, we believe that really structured clothes are beginning to enjoy a revival. Having worn the billowing swirls of summer crinolines, it's an exciting contrast to wear these grand and stately dresses that demand a more formal and sophisticated presence from the wearer.

Despite this antithesis, both Winter and Summer provoke in us our most creative designing, although of course every season offers us something special in the way of inspiration and occasions for which we can produce our special effects. Spring, Summer, Autumn and Winter—the four seasons of the year, and the four seasons of style. Although inspiration is such an intangible substance, and all designers find it hard to identify the many sources from which they draw their ideas, we've always been interested in remembering and recording images that have influenced us. On the following pages we've tried to convey how all these chance images come together in our designs, and our thoughts on style. From Marie Antoinette to Bianca Jagger, Winterhalter to Adrian, Bakst to Garbo, we look, remember and start to design. We believe that creating style and conveying it through our special effects is a fascinating and satisfying experience, and that everyone is capable of creating their own style.

Each season has its presiding spirit, the epitome of the time and the age, and each season builds up its own vocabulary of images to create a very definite style—the Emanuel style.

SPRING

*. . . luminous . . . fleeting . . .
. . . first love . . . fresh green . . .
. . . rosebud pink . . . last look
at childhood*

Spring

Spring is beauty emerging from the shell—beauty unadorned—like that of fourteen-year-old Marina Berni. We discovered this enchanting personification of Spring quite by chance, and were instantly reminded of the wistful innocence captured in so many Renaissance paintings of young girls.

Marina goes to school in London and attends ballet classes in her spare time, and, like any other teenager, prefers jeans, jumpers and boots for everyday life. But for a more special occasion, old-fashioned lacy dresses have a particular appeal for her. She was delighted with her finely pleated hand-tinted silk chiffon dress, and told us, 'I love it because it is very comfortable, it falls so nicely, and I can hardly feel it—it's so light and delicate.'

Thoughts on a Botticelli theme... we have always been intrigued by the diaphanous Greek-revival draperies and lissom beauty of the figures painted in the fifteenth century masterpiece, *Primavera*. Translating these Renaissance muslin draperies into modern terms has proved a challenge, and to reflect this mood we have made a number of dresses in the finest silk jersey, in Fortuny-esque pleated silk, and in the filmy transparency of hand-tinted chiffon.

Once we have defined a mood we can translate it into many different styles, to suit the many different clients we dress. One of our favourites, Susan Hampshire, has an elusive, springtime elegance, and we made this Botticelli-inspired dress for her in a pale shell-pink silk chiffon, frilled and elasticated with deceptive simplicity.

Spring

Young brides are a joy to dress. We can bring all our Botticelli effects into play and work in almost translucent fabrics, building up layer upon layer of transparent silk chiffon, and garland the bride with tiny spring flowers. Transparent layers conceal everything, but create a wonderful lightness. This dress, for example, is in white silk tulle and both the wedding dress and the bridesmaids' dresses are now part of the permanent costume collection at the Metropolitan Museum in New York.

We have aimed here at a rippling, wave-like effect; a very young bride has a delicate, fugitive beauty which could be destroyed only too easily if we were to design a richly elaborate, strongly-shaped dress for her.

36

Style for all Seasons

Spring 37

For Spring, simplicity is everything, as our daughter Eloise demonstrates, in her own interpretation of the Botticelli effect, in shell-pink elasticated chiffon, reminiscent of the dainty magic of Cecily Mary Barker's famous 'Flower Fairies' and the naughty glow of quattrocento cherubs.

Some to the sun their insect-wings unfold,
Waft on the breeze, or sink in clouds of gold;
Transparent forms, too fine for mortal sight,
Their fluid bodies half dissolved in light,
Loose to the wind their airy garments flew,
Thin glitt'ring textures of the filmy dew,
Dipt in the richest tincture of the skies,
Where light disports in ever-mingling dyes.

ALEXANDER POPE

A study of Renoir's many portraits of children of the French bourgeoisie in the nineteenth century reveals that he captures, perhaps more successfully than any other painter, the spirit of girls poised on the brink of adulthood, as can be seen in these two fine paintings: *The Children of Catulle Mendes* (right) and *Madame Charpentier and her children*. They are dressed as children, not as young adults, a principle we keep in mind when we are dressing very young girls.

Opposite: Princess Michael of Kent with her son, Lord Frederick, shortly after his birth. The mother and child theme has been an inspiration to painters throughout the ages. The innocence and the pleasure of a mother and child together create an inner harmony and serenity which we in turn like to reflect in delicate dresses of a like simplicity and purity. The Princess's statuesque good looks might have been an inspiration to the nineteenth century painter Franz Winterhalter. She always looks splendid in whatever she wears and has unerring style. She was photographed by Lord Snowdon in a white embroidered dress we made for her about three years ago.

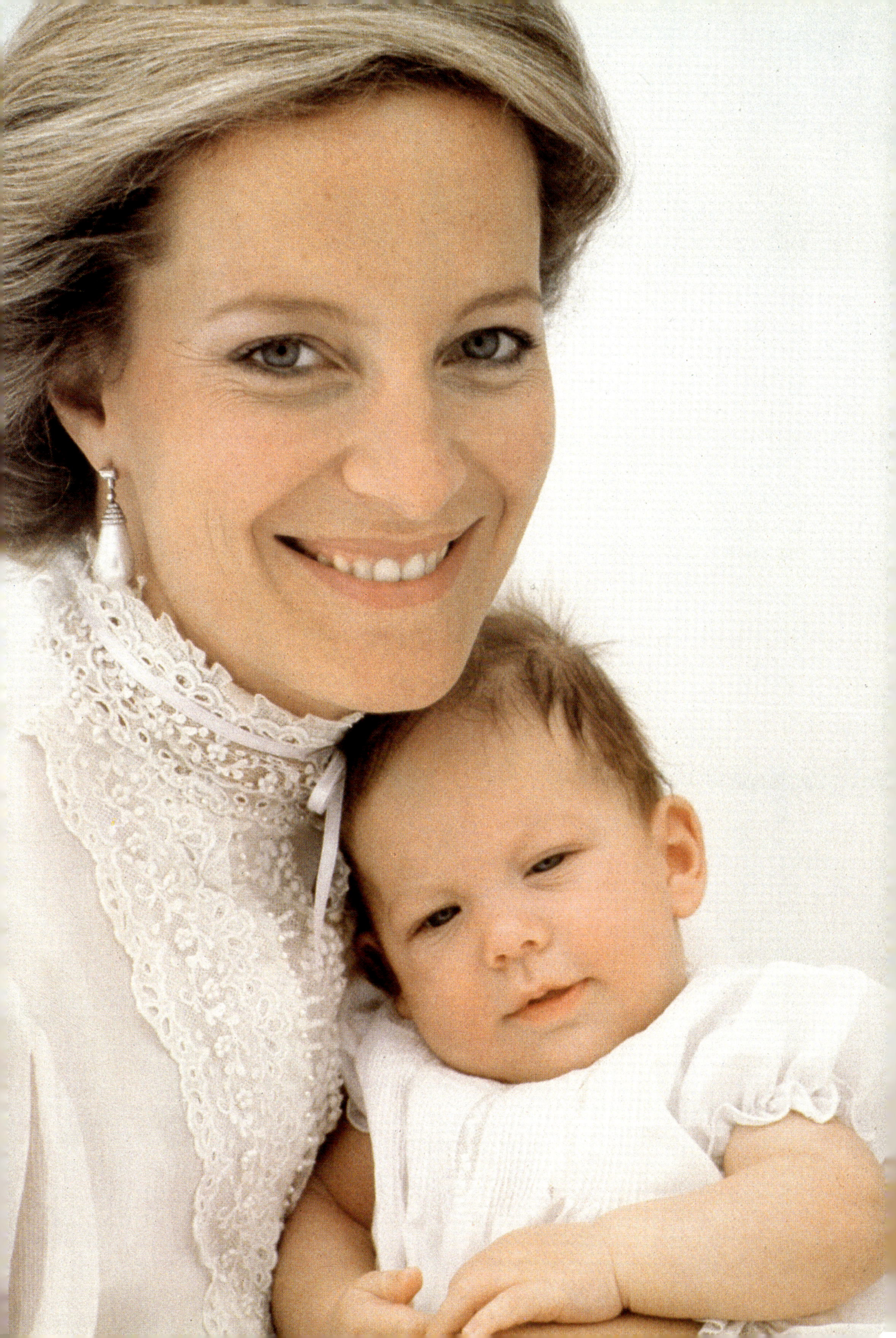

T wo little dancers from very different eras and backgrounds. Renoir's *The Dancer* (above, left) is a grave child, perhaps a little old for her years. She takes her ballet and her dress very seriously! Some fifty years later, the childish figure of Shirley Temple (above, right) is more accessible. There is none of the aloofness of Renoir's child ballerina. The tiny star is aware of her appeal and exploits it. But the two dancers do have something in common—both of them show off their dresses to perfection. In the time that separates these two very different images, the convention of the dance, or indeed party dress, for the little girl has hardly changed, as you can see from the picture of Clementine Hambro (right) and the small child and her mother (below, right). These dresses, to be effective but not heavy, should be built up of transparent layers of tulle or net to create a light effect which does not swamp the personality of the little girl.

A sense of scale and fitness is really vital when designing dresses to be worn by mother and daughter, as we are quite often asked to do for paintings. These used to be called, rather charmingly we think, 'picture frocks', and the child's version is not only scaled down, but conceived more simply and more childishly than that for the mother.

Spring 41

The ballet has been a fruitful source of romantic inspiration to us ever since we became aware of the beauty of late nineteenth century costumes. Looking at paintings by Degas and Renoir, or photographs of Pavlova in her many exquisite costumes, has helped to add detail to our repertoire of ethereally romantic designs. Every small nicety, for example the way Bakst festooned white muslin with pink silk roses, helps to build up to the final effect.

The lovely lightness of pure white classical ballet dresses inspired this net dance dress for a teenager. It's unashamedly romantic and perfect for dancing barefoot on the lawn!

Spring

Anna Pavlova as Giselle in 1903, and (below) in her favourite costume of white muslin, trimmed with garlands of pink silk rosebuds. Photographed in Berlin in 1908, this dress was designed for her by Leon Bakst and was probably the first of his costumes to be seen in the West as it predates the earliest performance of the Ballet Russe in Paris by about five years.

The two faces of the teenager: demure and shy, not really ready to emerge from the chrysalis—and, in contrast, the dare-devil disregard for convention. Teenagers do not want to treat clothes too seriously, and why should they, when they seem to be able to create marvellous effects for themselves without any apparent effort? Punk fashion, safety pins and all, is a typical expression of teenage love of rebellion, often for its own sake. We have always found this somewhat off-hand attitude very interesting—dressing the nonchalance of youth in a calculated style can result in some unusual effects. We particularly like the way English *Vogue* recently photographed a series of our net ballgowns with tiaras gleaming in spiked hairdos, as this is just the way our teenage clients like to see themselves.

Our crystalline dance dress (opposite) was directly inspired by costumes worn by Pavlova, and we find that variations on this ethereal theme remain extremely popular.

Spring

Style for all Seasons

Spring

One of our favourite pictures of a teenager is this affectionate portrait of Lady Sarah Armstrong-Jones, taken by her father Lord Snowdon.

She is wearing her royal bridesmaid's dress of ivory silk taffeta and lace, which was designed to complement the Princess of Wales's wedding dress. It is a teenage version of the royal wedding dress and was developed from the same basic ideas, but designed on a smaller scale. As head bridesmaid, Lady Sarah did an incomparable job keeping the little ones in order. The serenity captured by her father in this picture was much in evidence on that unforgettable day.

If any two dresses could be called 'signature' dresses, then these are the two we would choose to stand for the Emanuel style. They were part of our first collection, shown at the end of our Royal College years and they represent the solution to a problem that every designer shares—to create something— some handwriting— unique and recognisable. It is very much like being a painter or a writer. How do you acquire a personal way of seeing things and then translate it into a painting, a piece of writing, or a dress? We seemed to be attracted to ballet costumes from the last century, and particularly from the early period of Diaghilev ballets. The startling immediacy of the first impression, reinforced by myriad delicate details is essential in successful ballet design, and the same 'double-take' is really the key to the Emanuel effect. The overall grand design, never in a heavy fabric, is pointed up by the detailing . . . the rosebuds . . . the mother of pearl sequins . . . and the hand-embroidered lace.

Spring

Cecil Beaton, whose own cultural roots were firmly embedded in eighteenth and nineteenth century romantic revivalism, has also been a strong influence. The photograph (right) of his younger sister, Nancy, taken in 1926, has an Ophelia-like quality to it, and may have been directly inspired by Millais' famous painting. Some fifty years later his photograph of one of our favourite clients, Bianca Jagger, in our silk tulle and lace dress, is perhaps more reminiscent of Garbo in *Camille*, and maintains Beaton's great sense of style.

Romanticism may go out of fashion, but it is never out of style, and in any history of twentieth century taste, Beaton's highly personal romantic irony must be considered as an important link between the Edwardian era and the eventual return of the romantic ideal in the late seventies.

Spring

Romance never left the silver screen. A thousand flickering images of pretty girls in lace and tulle bear witness. Here are two of the definitive images: Greta Garbo in the great tragedy, *Camille*, and Vivien Leigh in one of the most romantic roles of all time, Scarlett O'Hara in *Gone with the Wind*. Scarlett's muslin barbecue dress has not survived, but this picture of it shows the influence of painters, such as Winterhalter, on Walter Plunkett, the costume designer.

The best Hollywood costume designers in the early days of the cinema researched period costume meticulously. They turned—as we do now—to paintings, museum costume collections, and contemporary engravings and prints for the basic information from which they could then build their designs. Their talent was to alter costume so that it had contemporary 'feel' to it and was thus more acceptable than something that simply had period charm.

They took a furbelow here and a detail there, studied corsets and busking, and produced designs of startling originality and allure. We are great admirers of the often underestimated work of Adrian, Travis Banton and Walter Plunkett. Their approach has influenced our work, both consciously and, we suspect, subconsciously.

Spring

Spring is the innocence of schoolgirls. It's allure unaware . . . or is it? Our recent series of tea dresses were designed as a response to this ambivalent innocence and inspired by the many pictures of Victorian children's clothes we've seen.

They are made up of layers of simple cotton lawn, built up in big frills and flounces and edged, rather like a Victorian handkerchief, with eyelet embroidery or with broderie anglaise. They are perfect for wearing on holiday in hot sunshine, but equally eye-catching as a younger alternative to the winter balldress.

Seen backstage at our last collection, the tea dress has the look of a young dancer waiting to go on and dance before a nineteenth century audience. Later, taken on location, the dresses look completely different, and have the aura of pioneer schoolgirls in Australia or perhaps in India at the turn of the century.

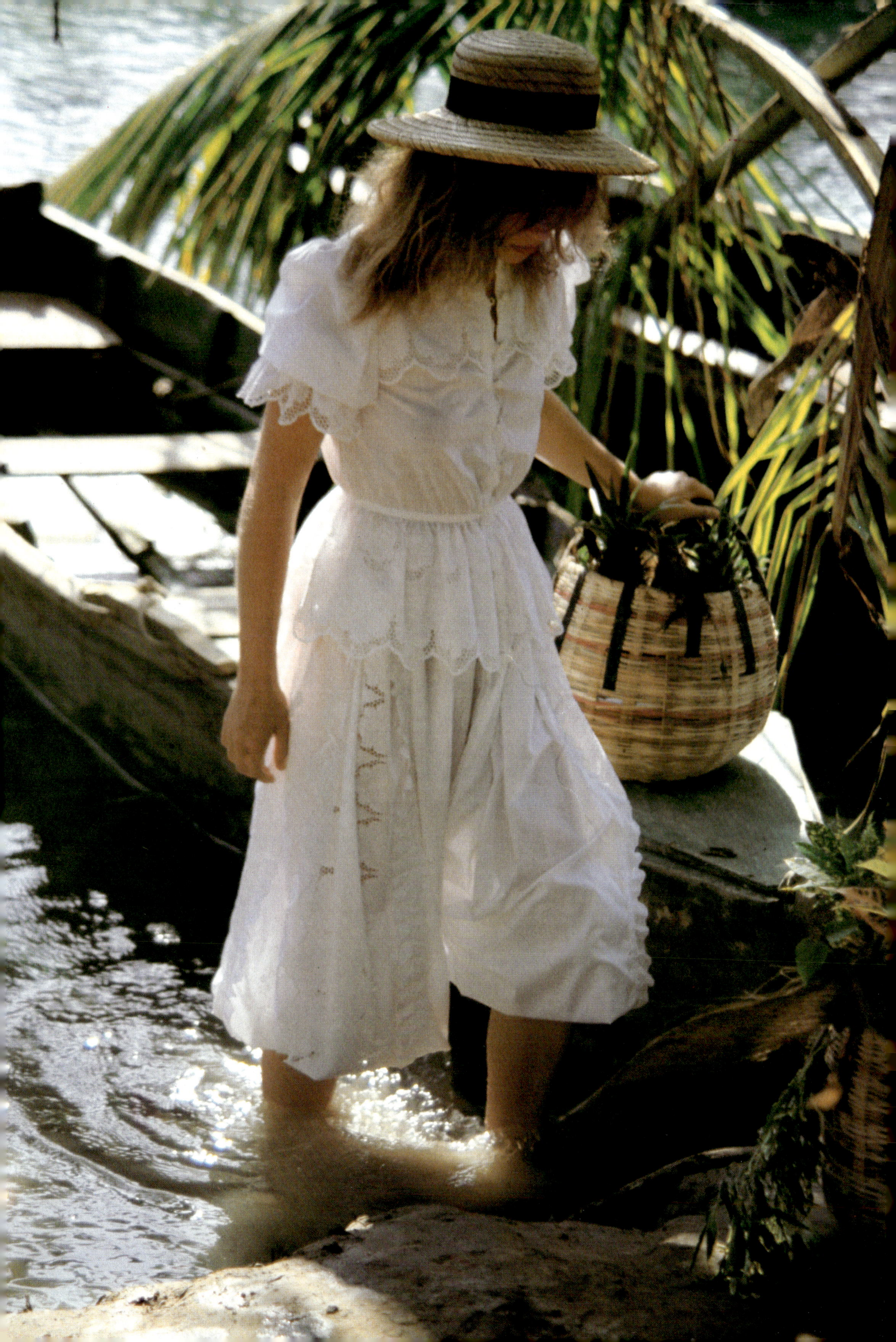

Style for all Seasons

Spring

We've also been inspired in creating dresses such as these by two films particularly rich in fashion 'atmosphere': Peter Weir's Victorian schoolgirl story, set in Australia, *Picnic at Hanging Rock*, and Roman Polanski's *Tess*. These prim white dresses create a provocative naïvety which has stimulated a number of ideas for designs. The first series we produced were so well liked that we are developing these designs further in different fabrics and effects, such as fine crêpe de chines, with hand-scalloped edging or inset embroideries, fine lace and even silk paper taffeta.

Susan Brooks is the promising young actress who has been chosen to star with Sir Ralph Richardson and Sir John Gielgud in *Invitation to the Wedding*.

We designed and made Miss Brooks' entire wardrobe for this film and found endless scope for our imagination in the wonderfully complicated plot, which includes three wedding scenes, and a dreamlike fantasy sequence where Miss Brooks wears an exuberant balldress while riding a large white horse.

This was our first venture into costume design for the cinema, and Miss Brooks' first starring role, and it proved to be a very happy and enjoyable association.

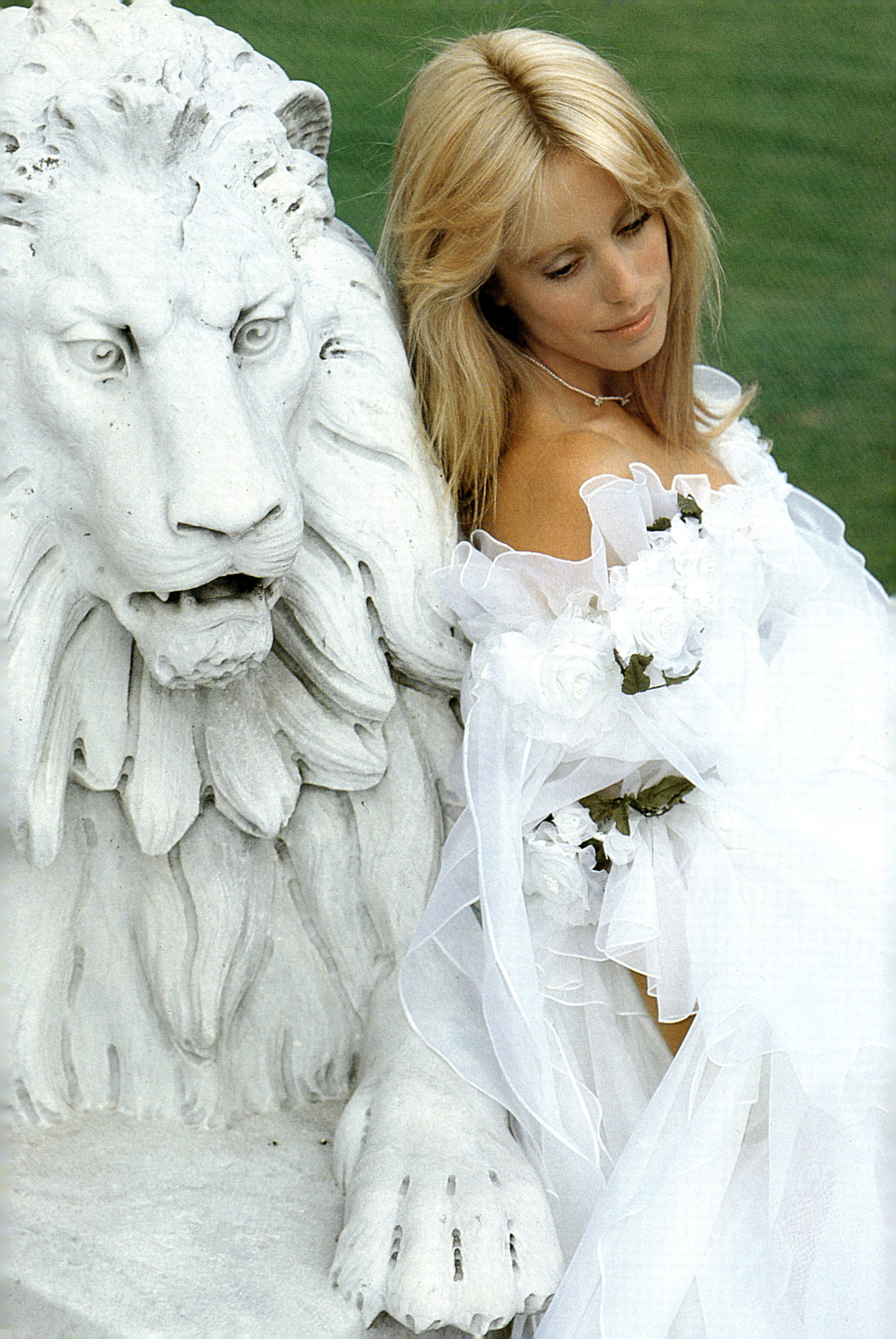

SUMMER

. . . pure light,
  pure white . . .
. . . flowers in full bloom . . .
  . . . butterflies on the wing . . .
far away romances

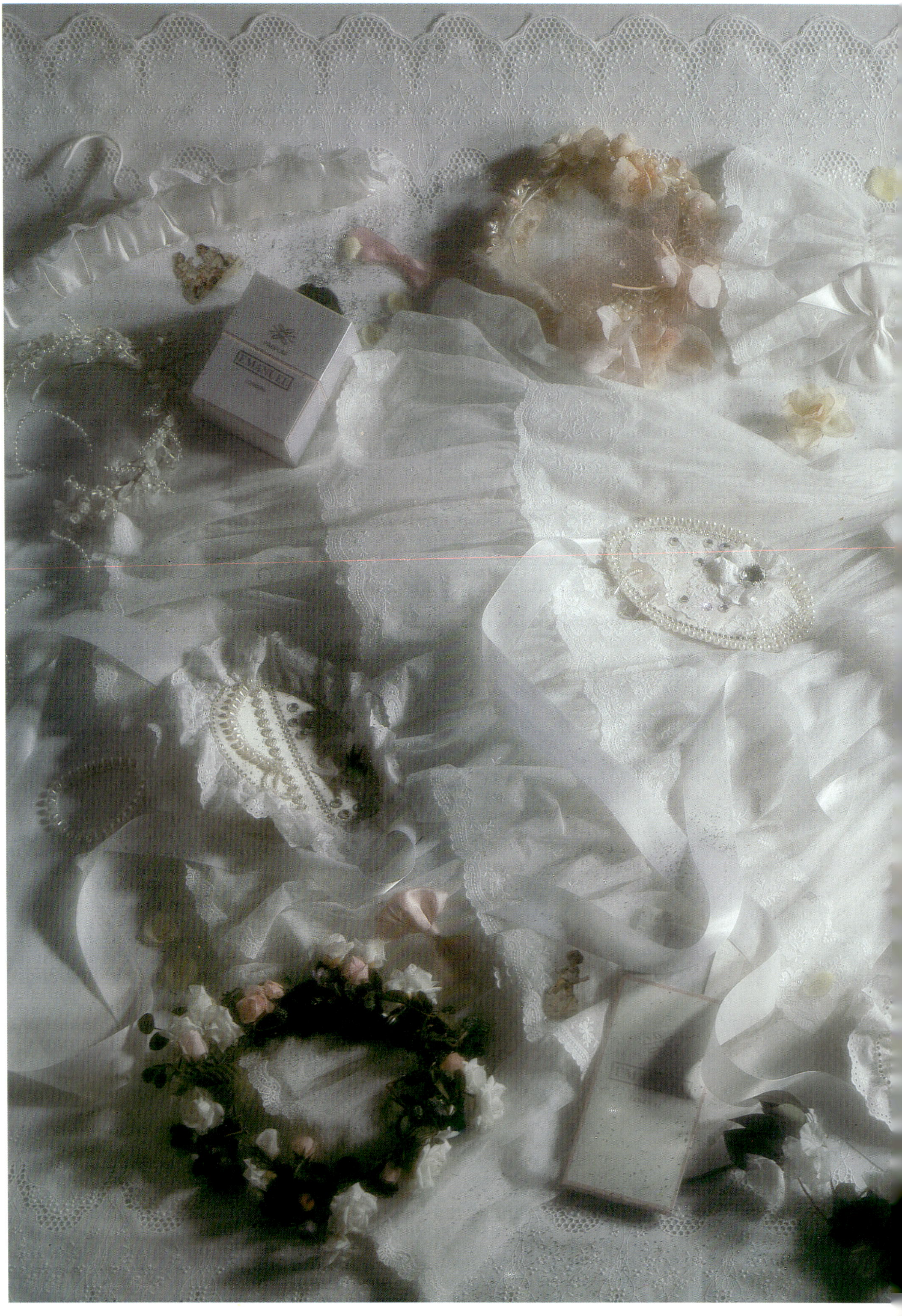
EMANUEL

Summer 63

Jane Seymour has worn our clothes before. She was presented to the Queen at the première of the film *The Four Feathers* in one of our earliest, post-art-school designs, a white paper taffeta dress inspired by the seventeenth century paintings of Sir Peter Lely, court painter to Charles II. She has a rather restoration face, we think, reminding us of paintings of Barbara Villiers and Frances Stuart with her subtle, slanting eyes.

'I buy romantic clothes wherever I go in the world, and love the romantic style,' she says. 'The earliest things I own were made in about 1790 and I still wear them, but I have been collecting for years and years and have examples from the thirties and forties as well as from Victorian times.' The dress she wears here is in ivory tulle, trimmed with roses and is, in her own words 'Pure fantasy, the absolute romanticism I love to wear. It reminds me of dresses I've been wearing for *The Scarlet Pimpernel*, in which I play the eighteenth century lady of fashion, Lady Blakeney.'

With her long gleaming waterfall of hair, her English rose complexion, and her love of *haute romantique* dressing, Jane Seymour is not only one of Britain's most beautiful and accomplished young actresses, for us, she is the very spirit of high summer romance.

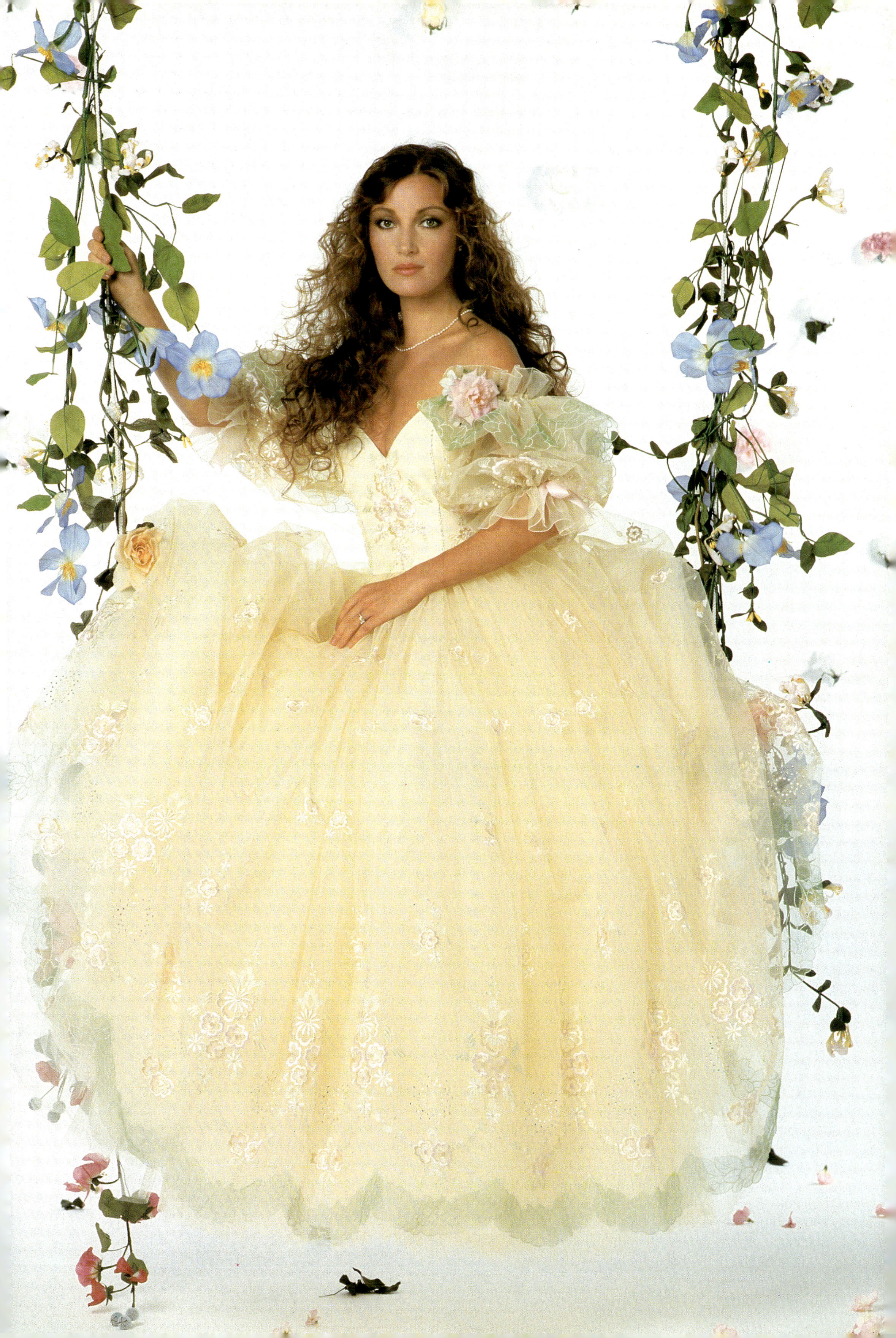

Summer . . . the time of dances . . . ethereal dresses floating over crinolines . . . full-blown roses and bare shoulders. Adrian's costumes for *Marie Antoinette* have never been surpassed in Hollywood for their precisely accurate period detailing, and the lavish use of embroidery so intricate it might well have been embroidered for Marie Antoinette herself. The scene of the great ball is the high spot in this rarely-shown film and really sums up our inspirations for summer ballgowns.

Marie Antoinette was the most copied woman of her age, and her dressmaker, Rose Bertin, the most sought-after in Paris. Eighteenth century clothes were designed in a rather different way to the modern counterparts we design. The basic dress or 'robe' was plain, and the decorations—flowers, gauze, net and bows—were added to the basic shape so they could be rearranged or completely changed at will. We often wish we could find people nowadays who could make the exquisite trimmings with which Madame Bertin decorated Marie Antoinette's dresses! This portrait of the ill-fated queen is one of many by her court painter, Elizabeth Vigée-Lebrun.

Summer

Society in eighteenth century Europe was confident, cultured, and carefree — until the wave of revolution that shattered the ordered and charmed life of the aristocracy the closing decades of the century. Fragonard can hardly be rivalled in his evocation of the spirit of the age in his famous painting, *The Swing*. The young woman swings amid a of flowers, urns, butterflies and garlands of summer leaves. It is this epitome of carefree summer gaiety that we aimed to capture for Susan Hampshire in this rose-tinted chiffon dress we designed for her.

Fragonard's painting has always had a strong influence on artists and designers, and Adrian's designs for Marlene Dietrich in *Scarlet Empress* (left) were notably rococo Filmed in the 1930s, it is one of the most elaborately costumed dramas ever made. Period detailing includes the butterfly sw effect of bows which was a typical eighteenth century device, first popularised by Madame de Pompadour at the French court, and subsequently copied by fashionable ladies throughout Europe.

A century later, opulence had returned on again to the French court under the Emperor Napoleon III, and the Empress Eugenie and her ladies (above, left) were painted in a scene of luxurious elegance by the society painter, Franz Winterhalter.

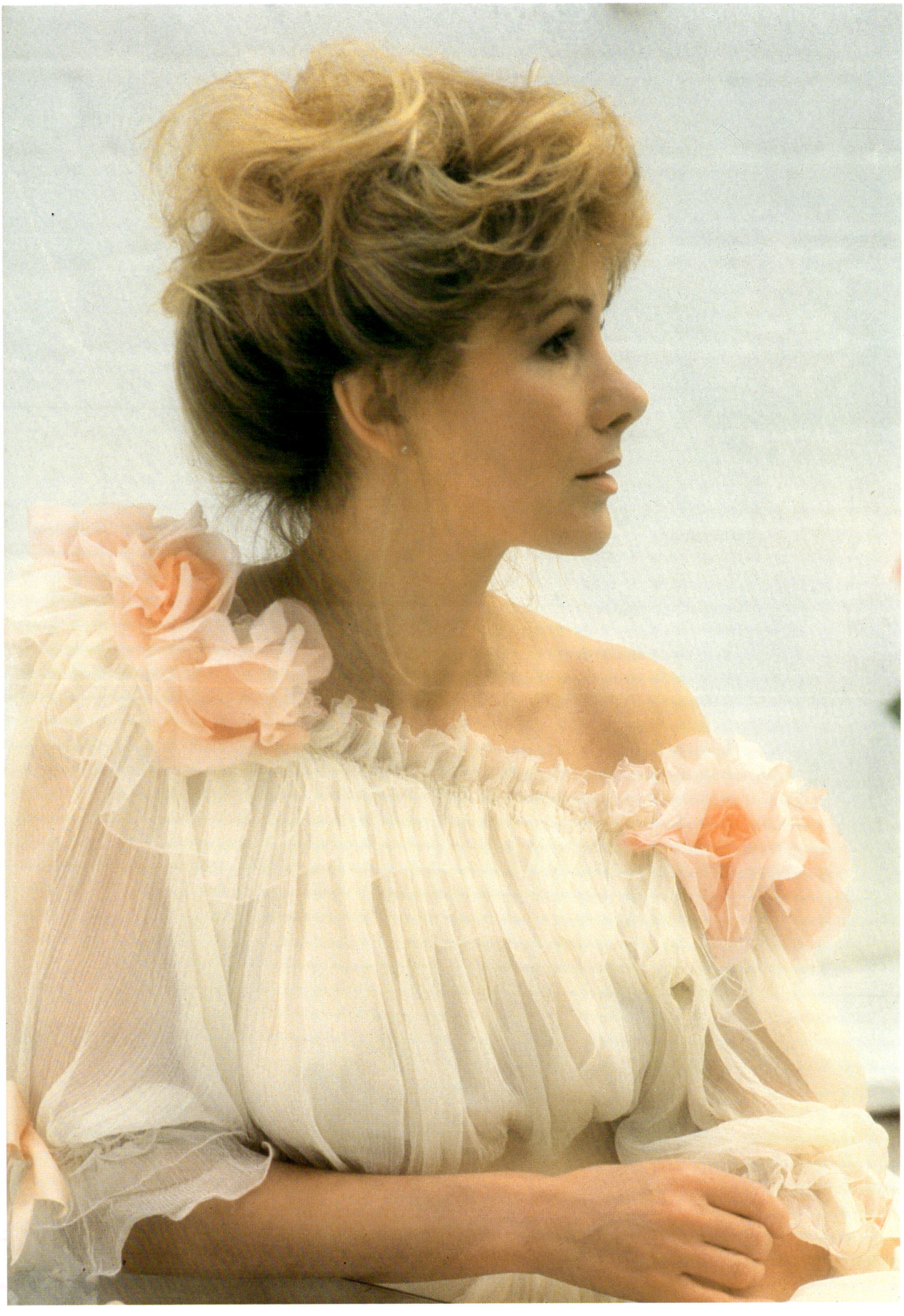

Portraits in picture frocks present us with a marvellous opportunity to make clothes that painters or photographers can make the most of. The concept of designing clothes to be painted (and today photographed) is long established. For a special feature in *Vogue* we recreated the mood of Summer suggested by an impressionist portrait by Renoir, *Madame Monet and her son*. The dress, in snowy chiffon with a lace collar and lace appliquéd bodice, was designed specially to echo the painting, and was photographed by Lord Snowdon.

In the early decades of this century the designer Lucile was famous for her dresses created solely to be worn for portraits, and this idea is once again acquiring popularity, particularly in the United States. We are frequently asked to design matching and co-ordinating children's dresses so that the whole picture presents a harmonious theme. We were recently commissioned to make co-ordinating dresses for this portrait of Kathryn, Lady Vestey with her two daughters, Saffron and Flora, painted by Carlos Sancha.

Summer

KATHRYN, LADY VESTEY & HER TWO DAUGHTERS, SAFFRON & FLORA

72

Style for all Seasons

Summer 73

The wedding umbrella
– in case of rain
Made of the same fabric as wedding dress and trimmed with lace, hand embroidered with sequins and pearls.

The pochette

Tiny golden horse shoe studded with diamonds – sewn into the dress for good luck

The wedding slippers –

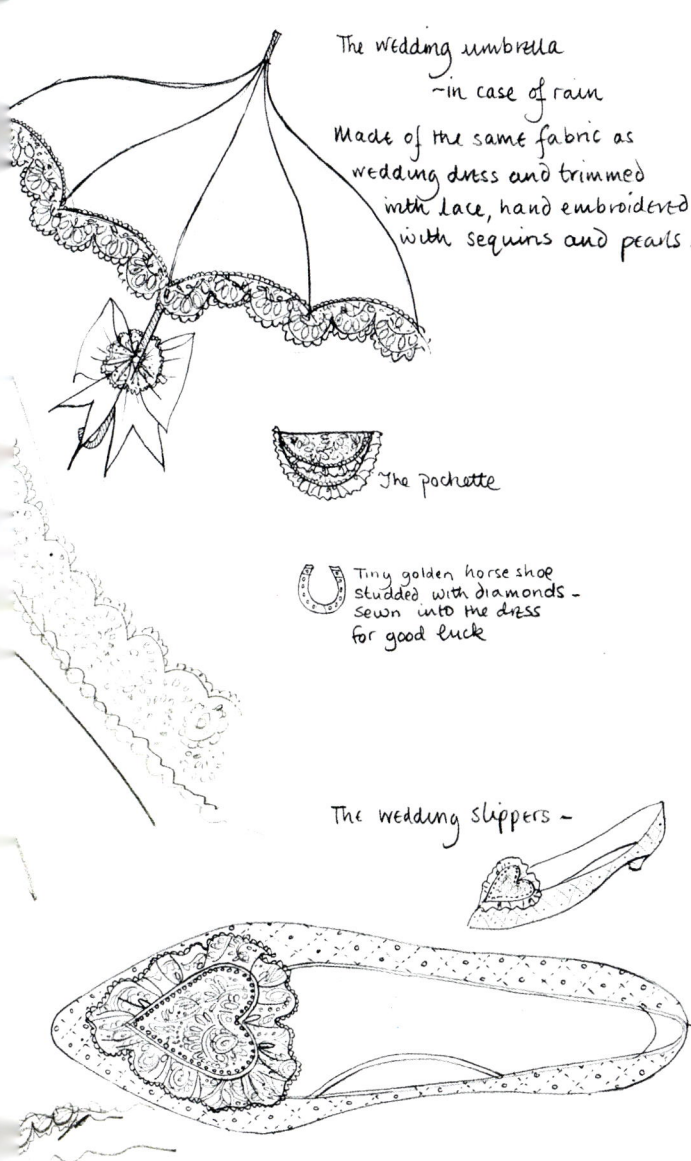

When we had the tremendous good fortune to be selected to design the wedding dress for the marriage of Lady Diana Spencer to HRH the Prince of Wales we kept one idea firmly in mind. Here, in the person of this beautiful young girl, was a once-in-a-lifetime opportunity to dress the fairytale princess on that most important day of her life. We wanted the dress to be every girl's fantasy wedding dress. We hope we succeeded.

We worked from very small initial drawings, keeping the grand design of the dress in our heads. This was partly for security reasons, but also because we had such a complete picture of the dress in our minds that we really only needed the tiny details on paper. We have drawn here our impression of the finished dress, based on our working sketches and on the rather simplified, diagrammatic drawing that was released to the world press on the morning of the wedding.

Details, as we have said before, are crucial when planning any wedding dress. We really do like to be involved in every aspect of the wedding group, as you can see from our drawings here of the Princess's accessories, and the dresses we designed for her bridesmaids, shown on the following page.

Style for all Seasons

Far left: Catherine Cameron; near left: Clementine Hambro—the two tiny bridesmaids who stole everyone's hearts. Below: from the official press release, sketches showing the original design for Catherine and Clementine, and, on the right, for India Hicks and Sarah-Jane Gaselee. Bottom: swatches of the fabrics used—ivory lace, ivory silk taffeta and gold silk taffeta.

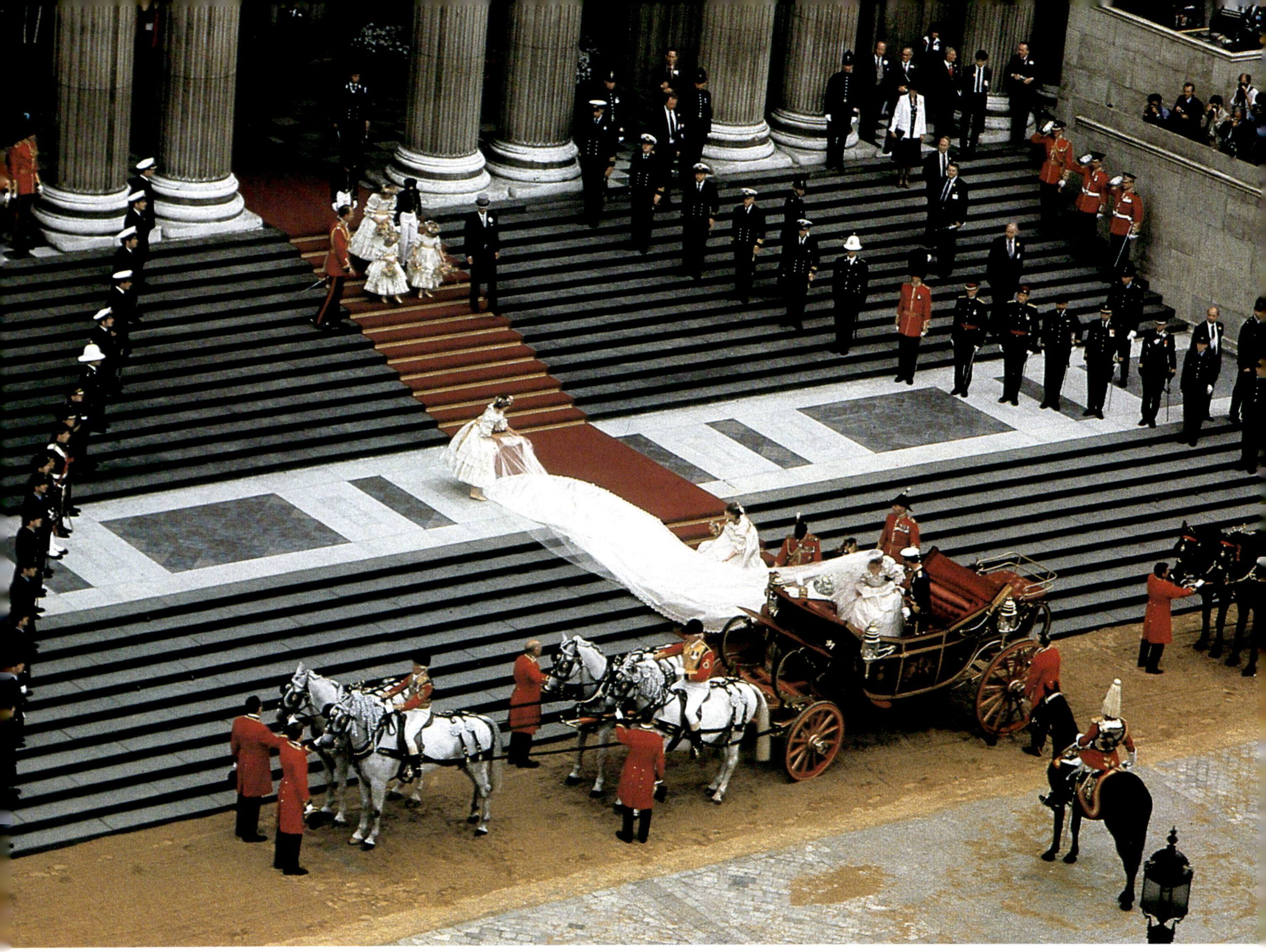

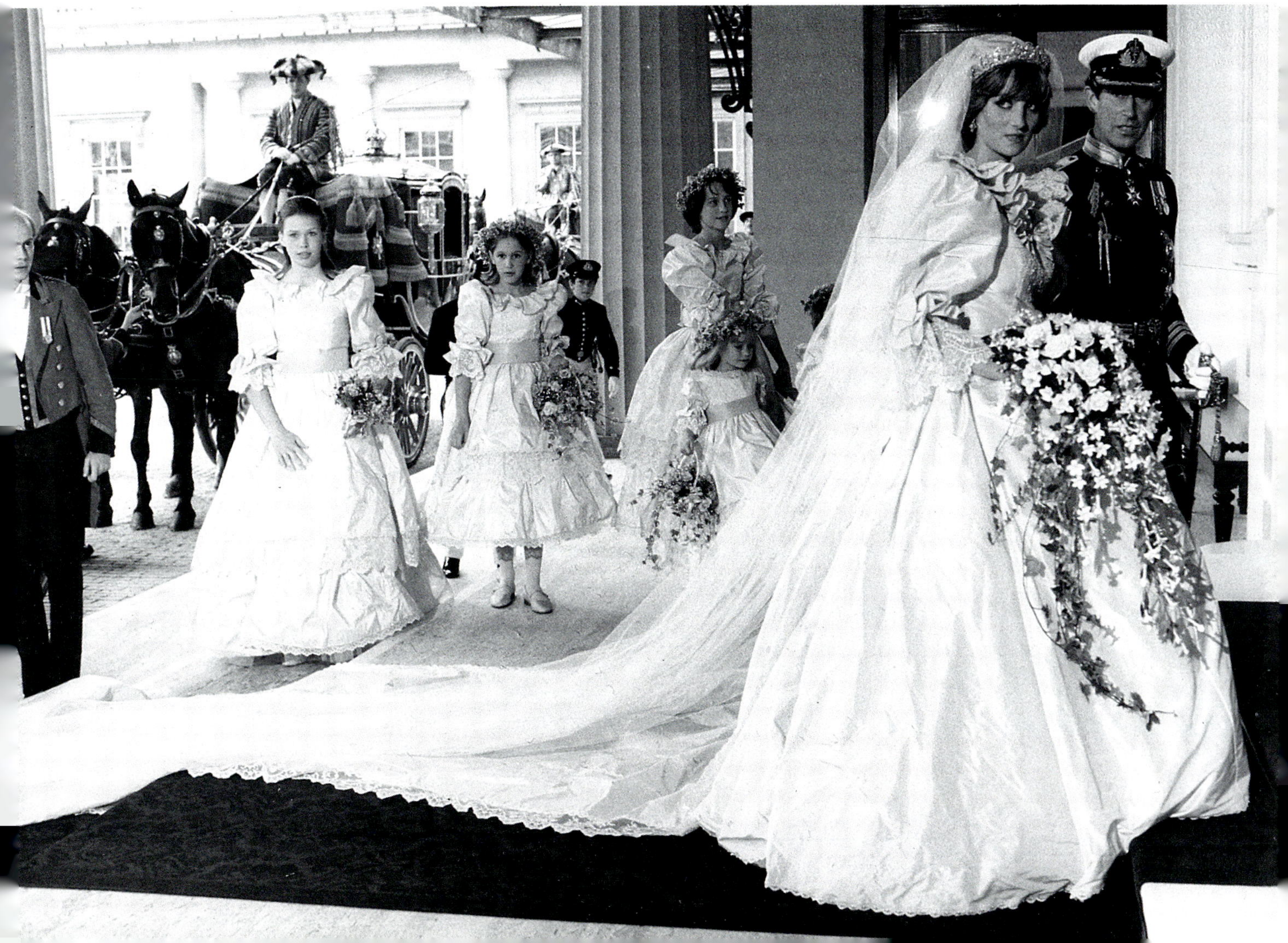

Style for all Seasons

Summer

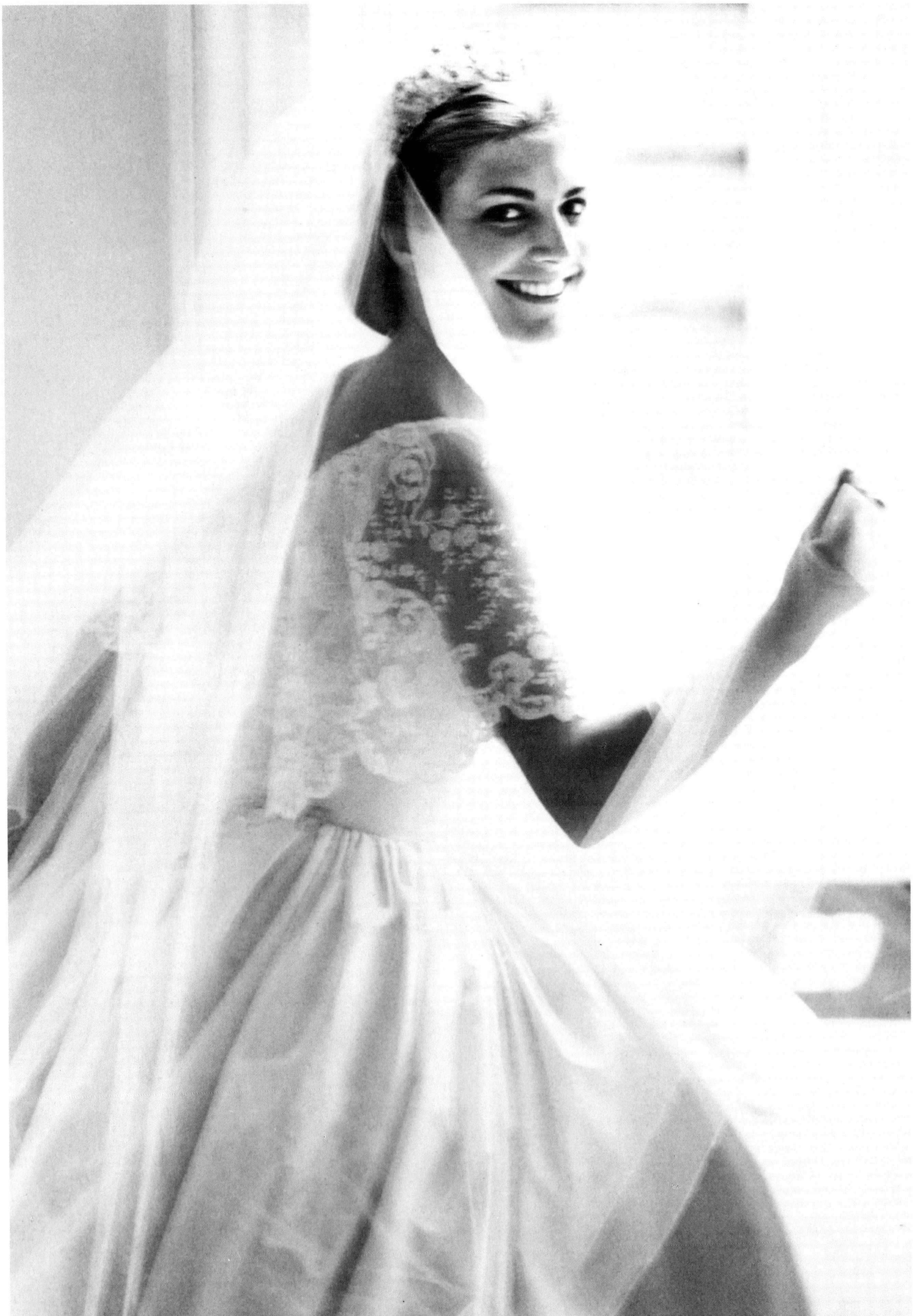

Summer

Two wedding dresses we have been particularly pleased with. Left: simple romanticism for Victoria Mancroft's dress for her wedding to Prince Nicholas von Preussen, and (right) iridescent sequins for Candia Wallop's wedding dress. We decided to make Candia's dress sparkle and glitter as she was being married in a very dark church and we were concerned that she should be seen easily by all her guests.

While the eighteenth century used bows as decorative devices, the nineteenth century fell in love with flowers: garlands, swags, single blooms, and tiny bouquets pinned to the bodice.

Apart from including fresh blooms in bridal bouquets, flowers have inspired us to create dresses based on buttercups, roses, poppies and lily of the valley. We use them in many different ways—sometimes sparingly in the form of tiny silk rosebuds for a child's dress, sometimes lavishly in the form of headresses, and sometimes to create a state effect—as we did for this wedding dress originally designed for a silk exhibition at Libertys, and now in the permanent costume collection at the Victoria & Albert Museum.

Flowers can be a frame for a face, or for a pair of beautiful shoulders; they can be clustered into a posy at the waist, or create a sleeve. We just cannot imagine there is any end to the ways of using flowers in our designs.

Summer

The Emanuel effect: close-up, the intricate detailing we work so hard to achieve is revealed. The beautiful piece of antique lace (below) was hand-tinted to a delicate shade of ivory, before being hand-embroidered with tiny pearls and mother-of-pearl sequins, finely tracing the intricate pattern of the lace. From across a ballroom, the effect is of points of light awash with colour. Opposite: the bride from our Pre-Raphaelite collection wears a dress of white silk organza spangled with tiny *diamanté*. Seen from afar the dress sparkles with reflected light, but close to, every individual stone becomes visible. The white satin corset, and the sleeves, are richly embroidered and jewelled in gold, pearl and *diamanté*, to create a romantic, fairytale wedding dress.

Summer

Style for all Seasons

Her Royal Highness The Princess of Wales, looking radiant in a slim dress of pale blue sequinned tulle, trimmed with pale pink satin bows and sash, is seen here attending a charity gala performance given by Welsh National Opera in Cardiff. This was her first official solo engagement in Wales following the birth of Prince William.

Opposite: A close-up of the talented and beautiful actress Patricia Hodge, in a sequinned and embroidered tulle dress—the subtle shade of green suited her colouring particularly well.

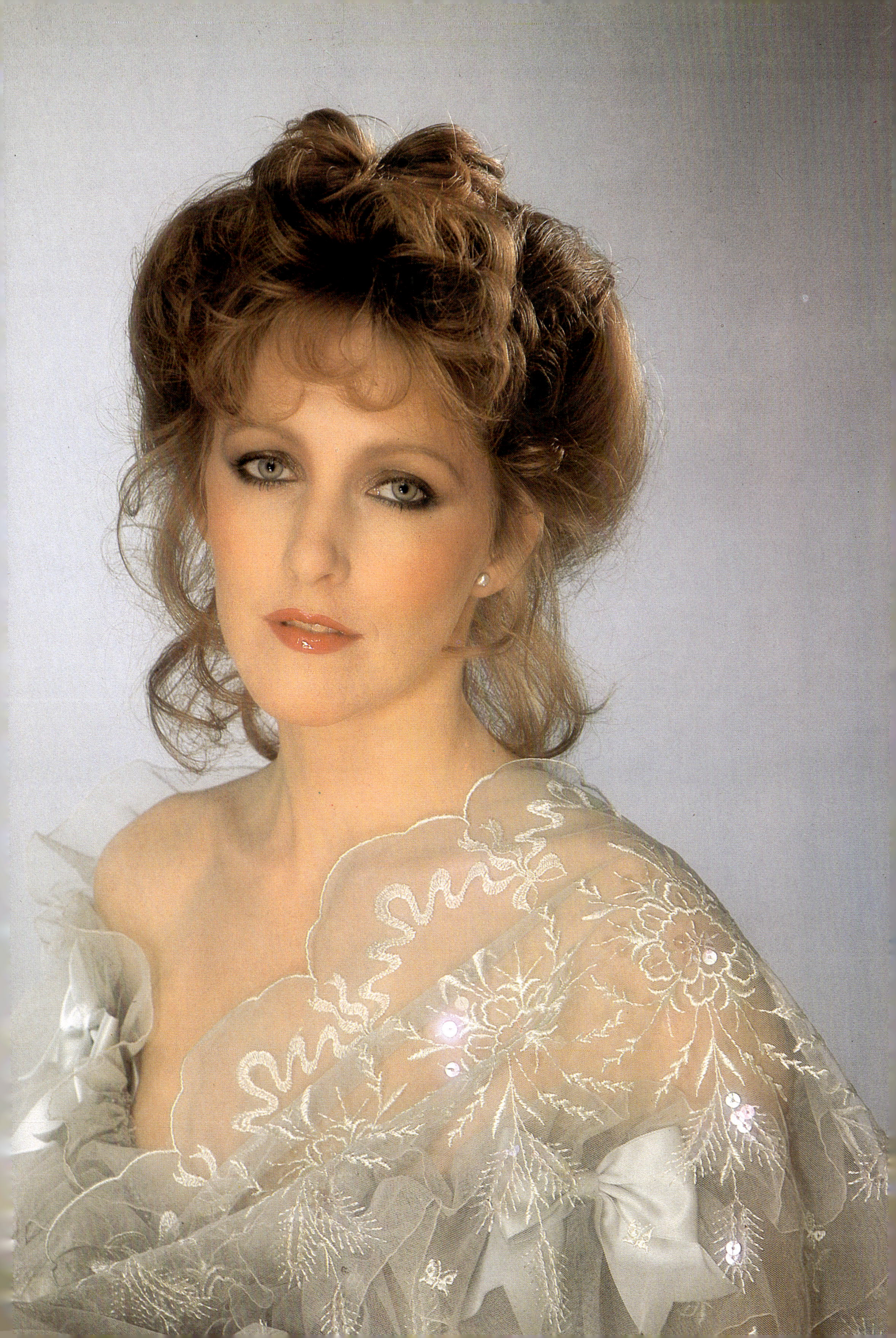

As an alternative to crinolines and airily transparent layers, we enjoy designing dresses for summer holidays. Silk jersey has always been one of our favourite fabrics. The effect is clean and spare, and it is as easy to wear as a soft T-shirt. We design entire wardrobes of clothes that can be packed into an overnight case, taken out, shaken out, and then worn in whatever combination the day demands. This is streamlined modern dressing and it works.

Summer

Bianca Jagger, who immediately brings a sense of style to anything she wears, is seen here in our white jersey summer dress, recreating a mood that owes a debt to Rudolf Valentino and *The Sheikh*.

Summer

Summer—long lazy days beside a pool . . . ice clinking in a long frosted glass . . . sunglasses and suntans . . . long sunsets and bright blue swimming pools. Swimsuits have to be dramatic to make an effect, and our recent designs in vibrant raw silks evoke cocktails and carnival in Rio. We bone the bodices, which are always strapless for an even tan, cut the leg up, and cut the backs right down for great exits.

There is a sort of primitive, jungle-maiden look about these effects . . . they could have been worn by Jane!

Style for all Seasons

Summer 91

Adding ruffles to soften the effect is a variation on the 'Jane' theme. Here, we commissioned this batik-inspired print to project a tropical jungle mood specially for exotic holidays. The perfect accessories? A banana leaf . . . a shady straw hat bought locally . . . and a long cool drink!

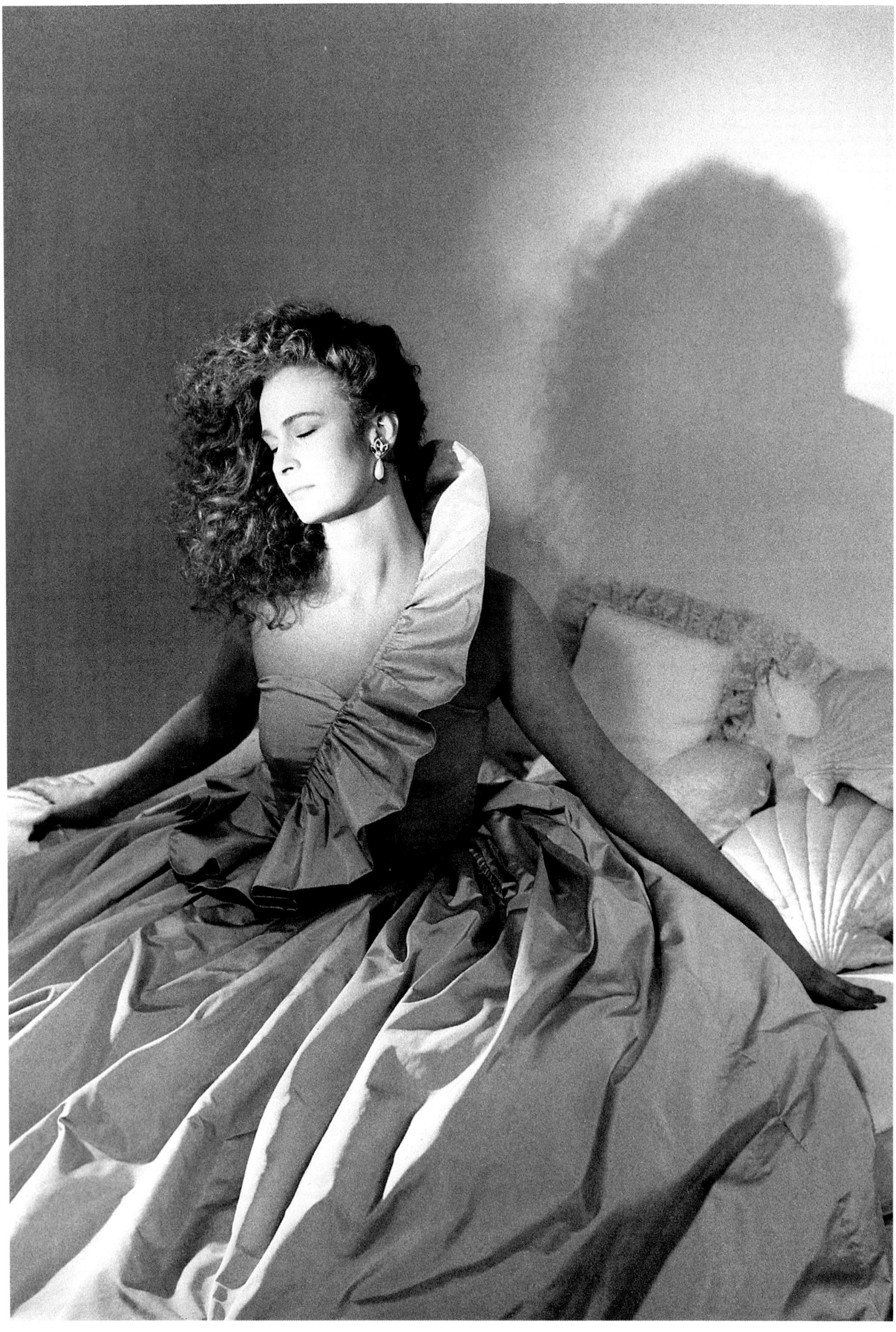

Stiff ruffles also look elegant when used for summer ballgowns. Princess Anne is wearing a ruffled taffeta dress in old gold, edged with lace, loaned to her especially for this portrait which was photographed by Lord Snowdon.

Taffeta again (left), in a smoky pink, is stiffly ruffled round the bodice for a more sophisticated summer evening look.

Style for all Seasons

Summer

Style for all Seasons

Summer

The silly season...when the big city is empty and newspapers have to hunt for stories... when the mood is carefree and fun... Summer in the city and why not on roller-skates? The Emanuel effect will go anywhere, on anything, as master photographer Norman Parkinson proves here in his essay on ballgowns ... which glide.

Style for all Seasons

Some people have a larger-than-life quality—and so do some dresses . . . something that places them in a superstar category.

Superstars are dramatic. Marlene Dietrich (right) and Carole Lombard (below, right) both had that sense of drama, which we have translated into the rather alternative wedding dress modelled by Marie Helvin, and the 'Vienna' dress on the opposite page, so-called because it was inspired by Strauss waltzes and mid-Victorian prettiness. Drama is a question of exaggeration, hyperbole perhaps, which some people, like Marie Helvin, carry off superbly.

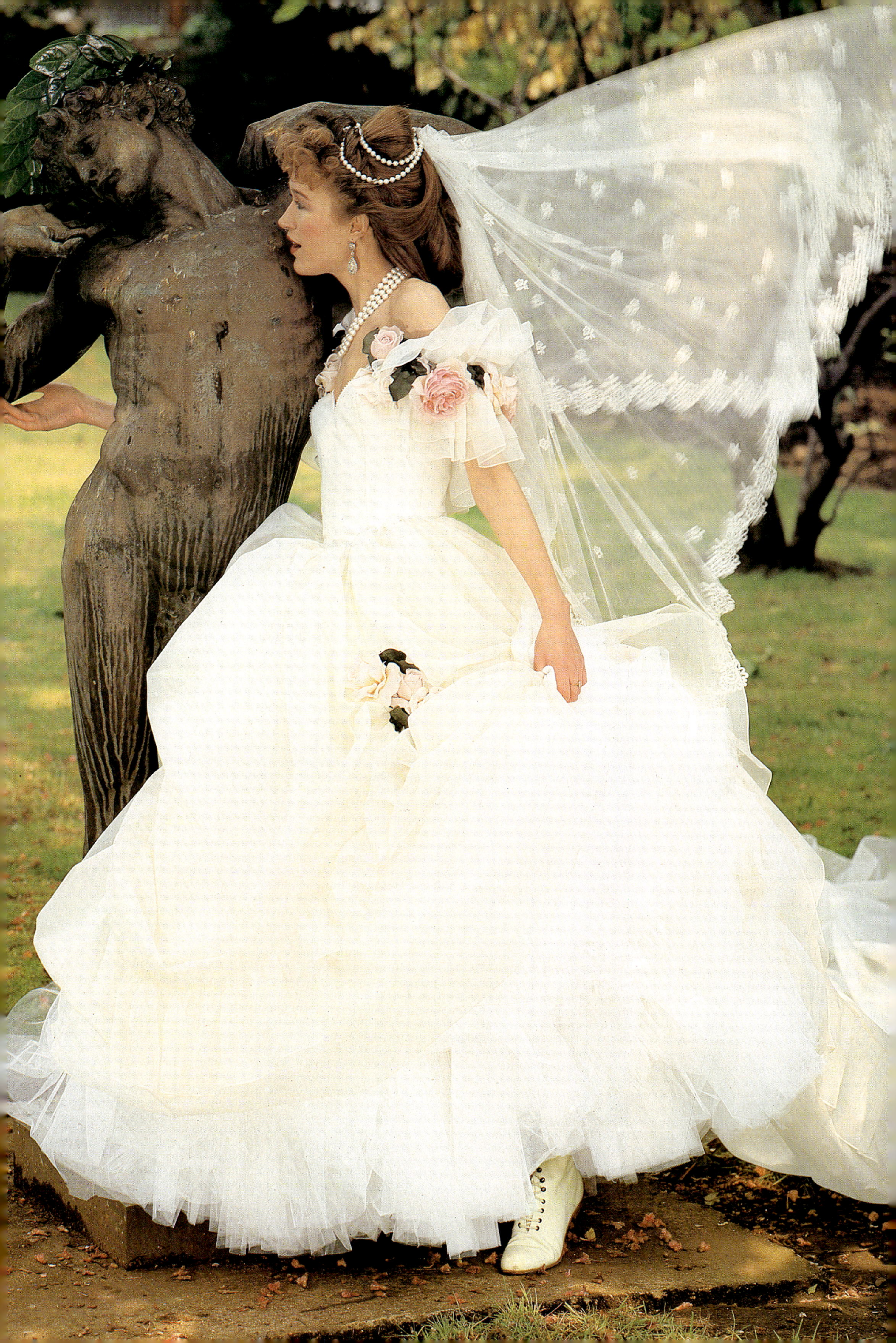

Style for all Seasons

Her Royal Highness The Duchess of Kent is a water-colour dream silver blonde. To dress someone who has her spirit of romance and charming spontaneity is a pleasure and a privilege.

One of our favourite clients, we have had occasion to design outfits for her which have included both formal and informal wear for engagements at home and overseas.

The Duchess of Kent lends a touch of personal style to everything she wears—never more apparent than in these two pictures, where we hope the dresses complement her air of elegance and fragility.

AUTUMN

. . . grand glittering nights . . .
. . . days of mists and leaves . . .
. . . jewelled fantasies . . .
fireworks of bronze and gold.

Style for all Seasons

Autumn

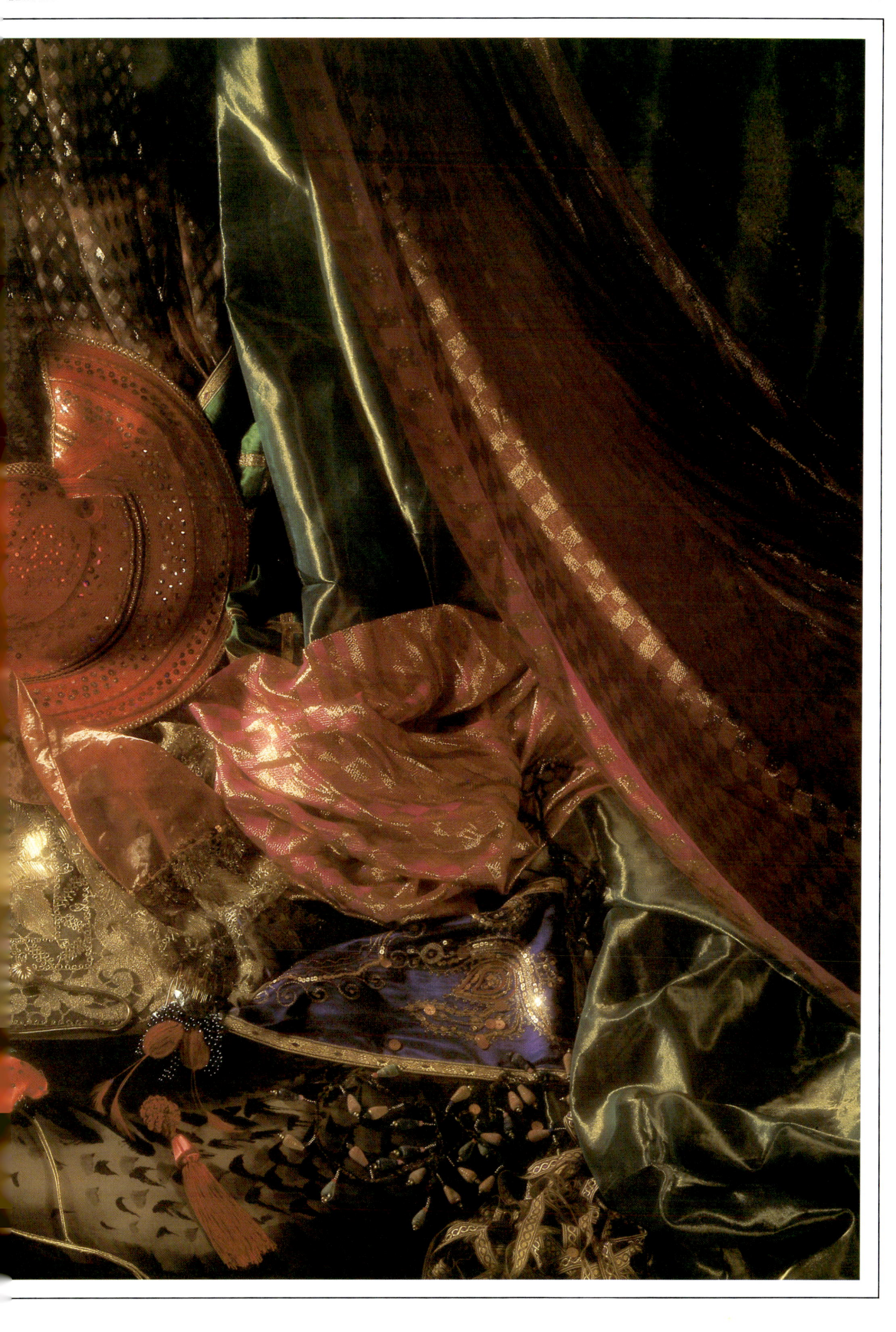

Bryony Brind, soloist with the Royal Ballet Company, is flamelike in her flickering movements. Hers is an elusive beauty . . . time is suspended as she moves and each shape she makes floats effortlessly from the one before. We have seen her dance, many times, notably as Nikiya in *La Bayadère*, with Nureyev. Here she interprets the spirit of Autumn for us in a dress inspired by the Pre-Raphaelites.

'I love this dress because it's the sort of elaborate and studied look that we wear in the ballet for court dances', she told us. 'In clothes like these you can become a different person. They help one create a character, to project something very different from oneself, because they are so definite.' Was it, we asked, difficult for her to dance the classic roles that had been made famous by ballerinas of the past such as Pavlova and Karsavina? 'No, not really. I enjoy it, because you bring your own personality to each role, even though it was created by someone else, but at the same time I do love contemporary ballet—it is such a tremendous challenge to create something entirely new. Of course, you move differently in different clothes—they almost dictate movement, particularly these rich, elaborate costumes, and this adds an additional dimension for me when projecting myself in the ballet.'

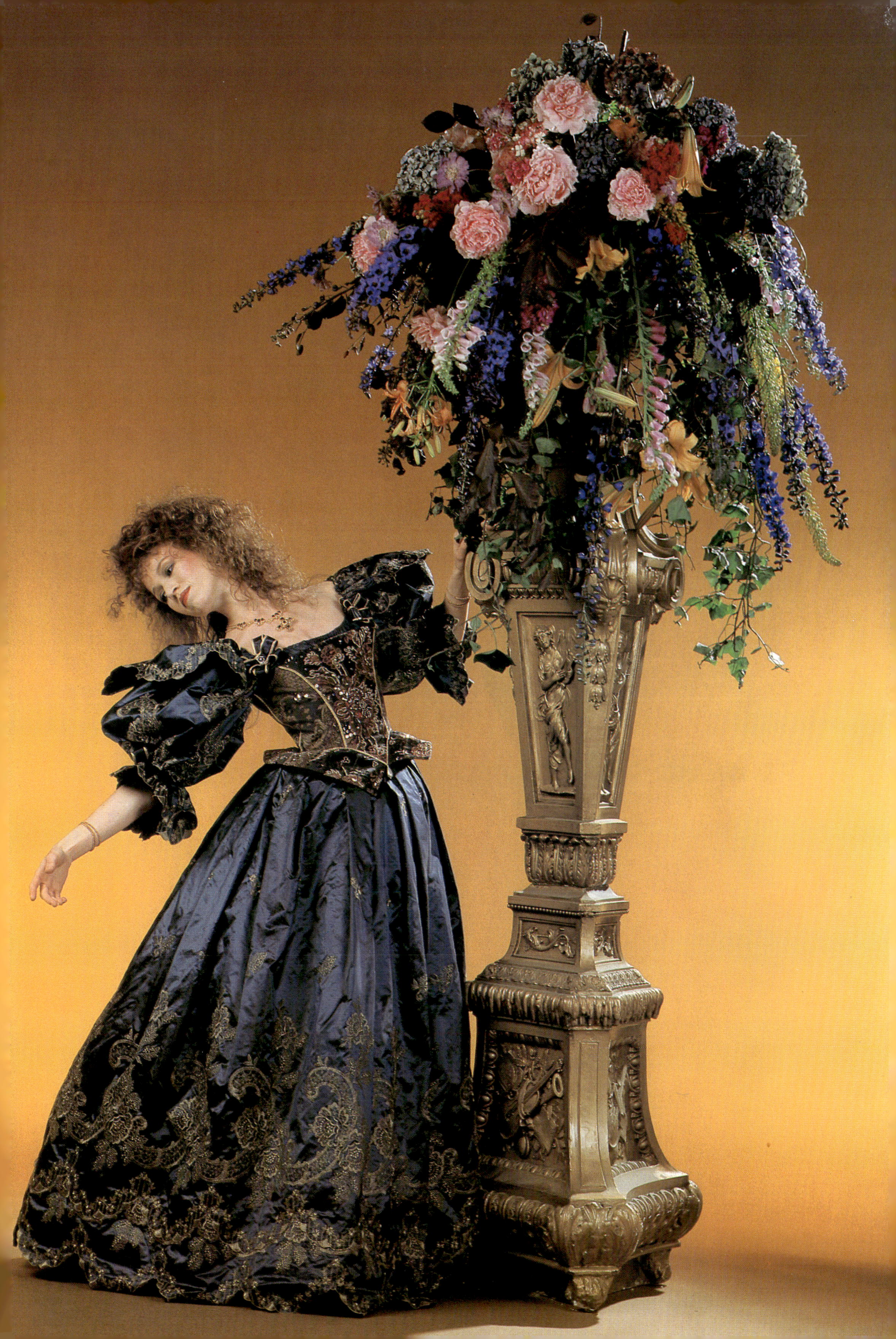

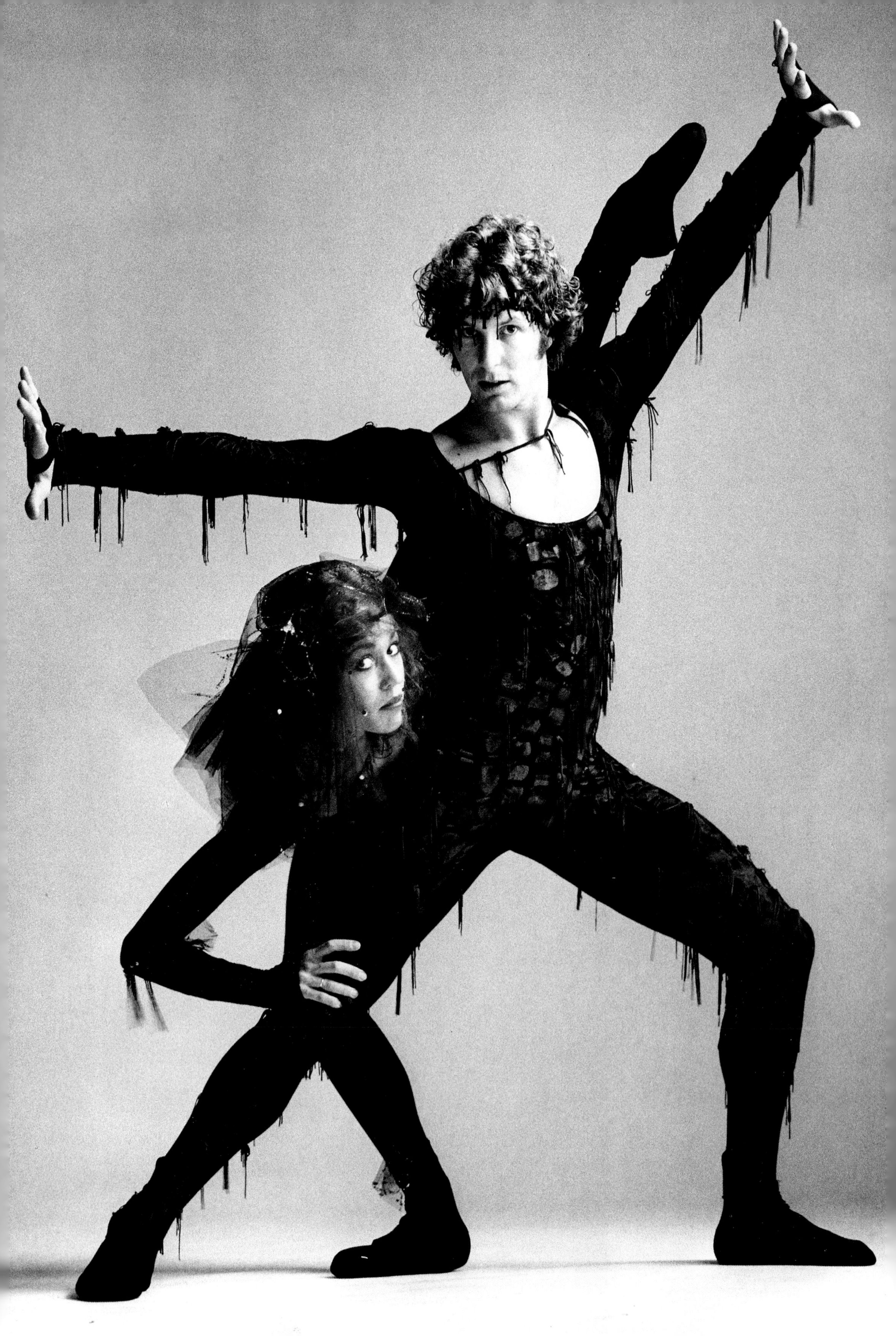

Autumn 109

Come into my parlour—said the spider to the fly...

Wayne Eagling and Bryony Brind dance the 'Deadlier than the Male' ballet, choreographed by Wayne Eagling, with costumes designed by us. These are the first ballet designs we've done, and remarkable effects can be obtained by using sequins, which shine like laser beams under the spotlights. Ballet design is really most successful when it reflects and magnifies movement, and we have had to rethink quite a few of our techniques, so that the costumes can withstand the tensions that such freedom of movement demands. It's a fresh and exciting challenge for us.

There will never be anything to equal Nijinsky's leap backward on to the stage at Monte Carlo, in 1911, as 'La Spectre de la Rose'. Inspired by this extraordinary moment in the history of the ballet are these preliminary sketches for a new ballet entitled 'Briory Rose'.

In designing for ballet, there is an inherent conflict between the fantasy effect that the audience sees and the practical realities of boning and hooking that the dancers must rely upon totally. We like to discuss our designs with the performers at a very early stage and work out costumes that will enhance the mood of the dance without inhibiting or restricting any of the choreography for the ballet.

La Spectre de la rose

Souleve ta paupière close
Qui effleure un songe virginal;
Je suis la spectre de la rose
Que tu portais hier au bal.
  Theophile Gautier

Autumn 111

Poison Ivy

Diaghilev's Ballets Russes have been a profound inspiration for our most fantastic effects. He was an extraordinary man, a svengali of every talent that contributes to a ballet and a man with an extraordinarily sensitive eye for colour and design. He himself never underestimated the importance of design in ballet: he was an absolutely committed modernist in outlook, as this excerpt from an unpublished interview with a reporter from *La Renaissance*, a Russian-language paper published in Paris clearly shows. The interview took place in 1928, the year before Diaghilev's death.

'If theatrical creativity is to evolve, it is not enough to remain faithful to our teachers. We were not taught algebra and ancient Greek in order to spend our lives solving problems or speaking the language of Sophocles. Today, dance and choreography must, of course, get their graduation certificate from the classical school, but only in the sense in which a Picasso must have precise knowledge of human anatomy, or a Stravinsky would be forbidden to write parallel fifths while he was still a student.'

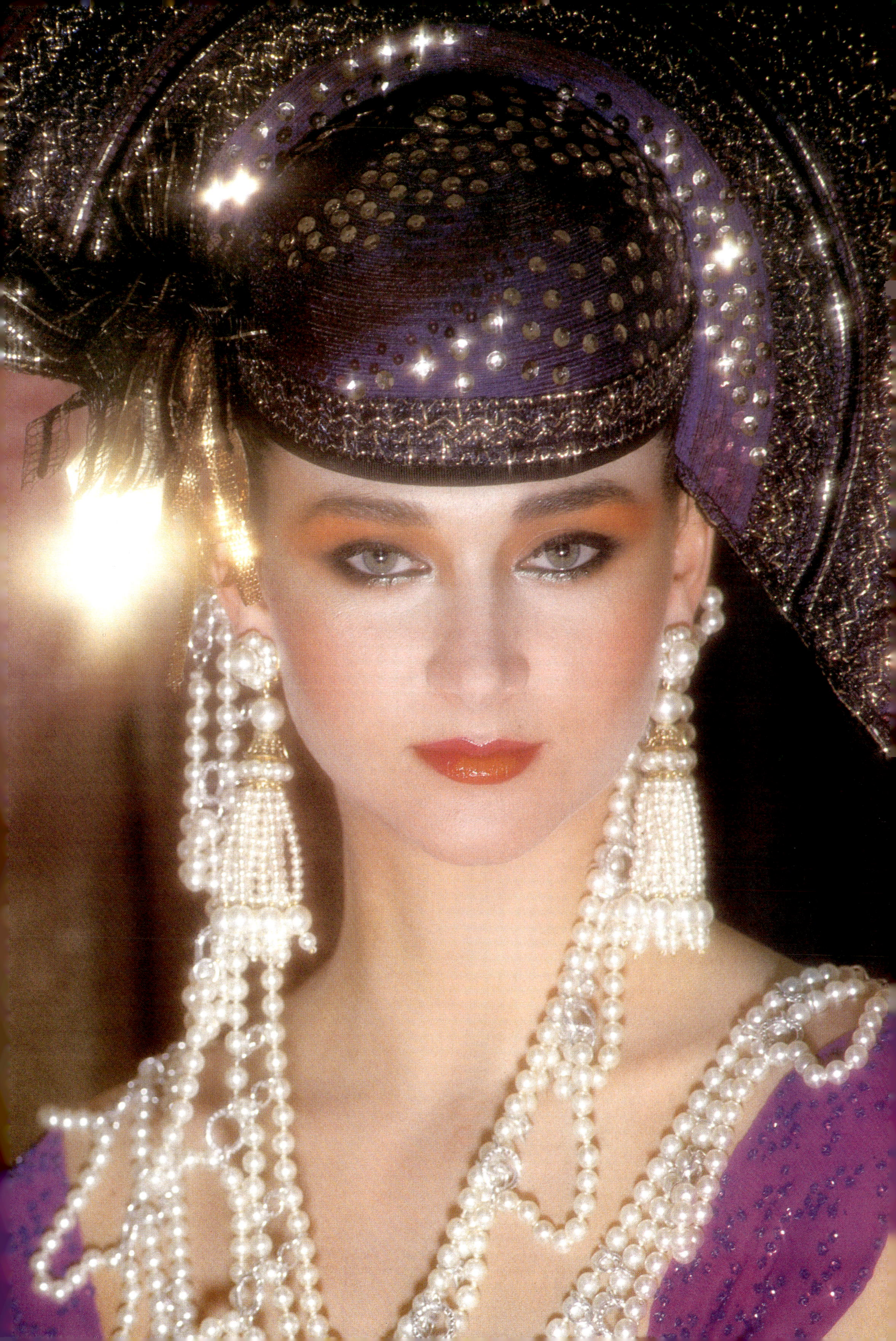

Style for all Seasons

The bearers set the casket down in the middle of the temple. Then four slaves began an astonishing manoeuvre. They unwound the first veil, which was red, with silver lotuses and crocodiles, then the second veil, which was green with the history of the dynasties in gold filigree; then the third, which was orange with prismatic stripes and so on until the twelfth veil, of dark blue, which, one divined, enclosed the body of a woman. Each veil was unwound in a different fashion; one called for a manege of intricately patterned steps, another for the skill needed to shell a ripe nut, another for the casualness with which one plucks the petals of a rose; the eleventh veil, in what seemed the most difficult movement, was peeled off in one piece like the bark of a eucalyptus.
Jean Cocteau describing Ida Rubenstein's appearance as Cléopâtra in 1913. Her costumes were designed by Bakst.

Autumn

Everything that dazzles, intoxicates and seduces us had been conjured up and drawn onto the stage, there to flower as perfectly as the plant world attains its magnificence under the influence of the climate.'

The 1909 première in Paris of the Ballets Russes, described by Countess Anna de Noailles, in 1930.

The dulled old-gold of autumn leaves contrasts with the watery brilliance of rose-cut diamonds for a net ball dress, inspired by the magnificent flowering of the Ballet Russes.

Autumn

Style for all Seasons

Our visit to India revealed a new world of rich, exotic fabrics: every sari shop we visited seemed to have the most amazing bales of gold tissue on display. Elaborate embroidery is not a rarity as it is in Europe, but an everyday elegance in India. One of the highspots of our stay was to discover the same transparent gold moiré tissue that Bakst had used so often when constructing his elaborate ballet costumes—particularly the oriental-influenced costumes for *Scheherazade* and *Cléopâtra*.

We bought a number of antique fabrics there, and our particular favourites were the elaborate panels of embroidery which are worn as skirts under saris. The Indians wear these so that only a narrow piece is used, visible from the front, so we bought several and pieced them together to make very full gypsy skirts. We now work with various fabric mills in India who make exclusive embroideries for us, using very rich silk threads. The workmanship is really exquisite and the vivid colours, which look so natural under the bright Indian sun, translate into splendid evening clothes for English autumns.

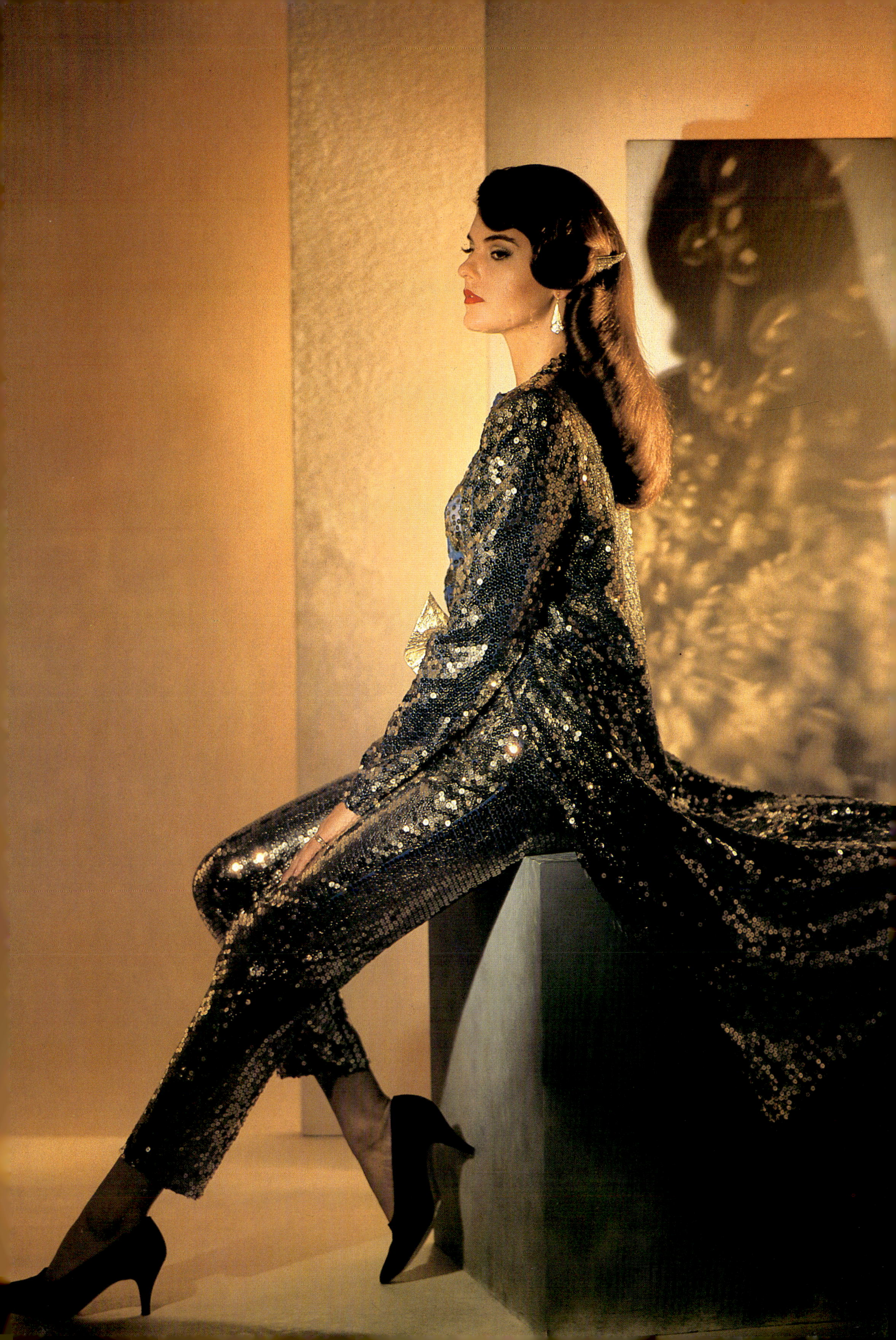

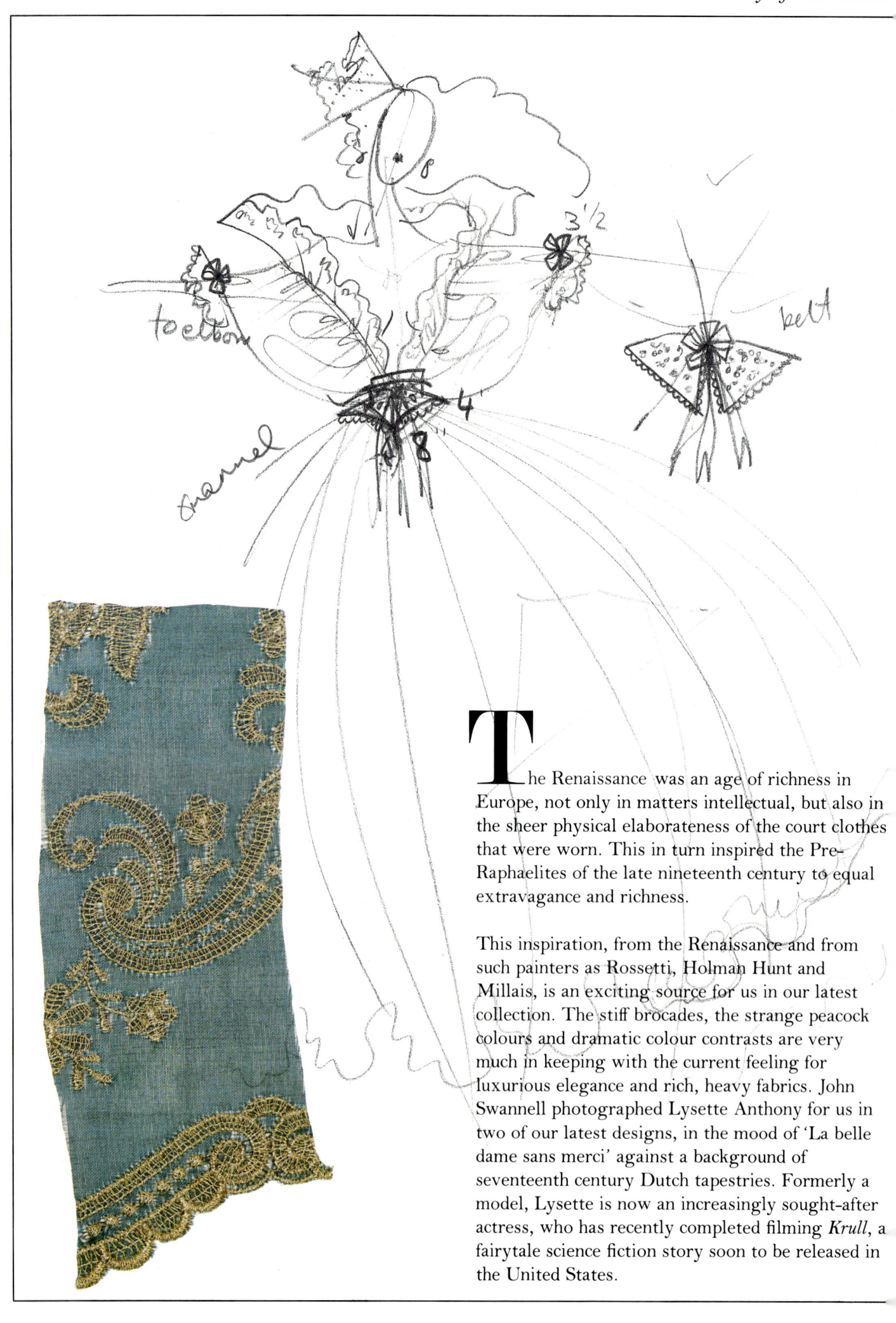

T he Renaissance was an age of richness in Europe, not only in matters intellectual, but also in the sheer physical elaborateness of the court clothes that were worn. This in turn inspired the Pre-Raphaelites of the late nineteenth century to equal extravagance and richness.

This inspiration, from the Renaissance and from such painters as Rossetti, Holman Hunt and Millais, is an exciting source for us in our latest collection. The stiff brocades, the strange peacock colours and dramatic colour contrasts are very much in keeping with the current feeling for luxurious elegance and rich, heavy fabrics. John Swannell photographed Lysette Anthony for us in two of our latest designs, in the mood of 'La belle dame sans merci' against a background of seventeenth century Dutch tapestries. Formerly a model, Lysette is now an increasingly sought-after actress, who has recently completed filming *Krull*, a fairytale science fiction story soon to be released in the United States.

Autumn 121

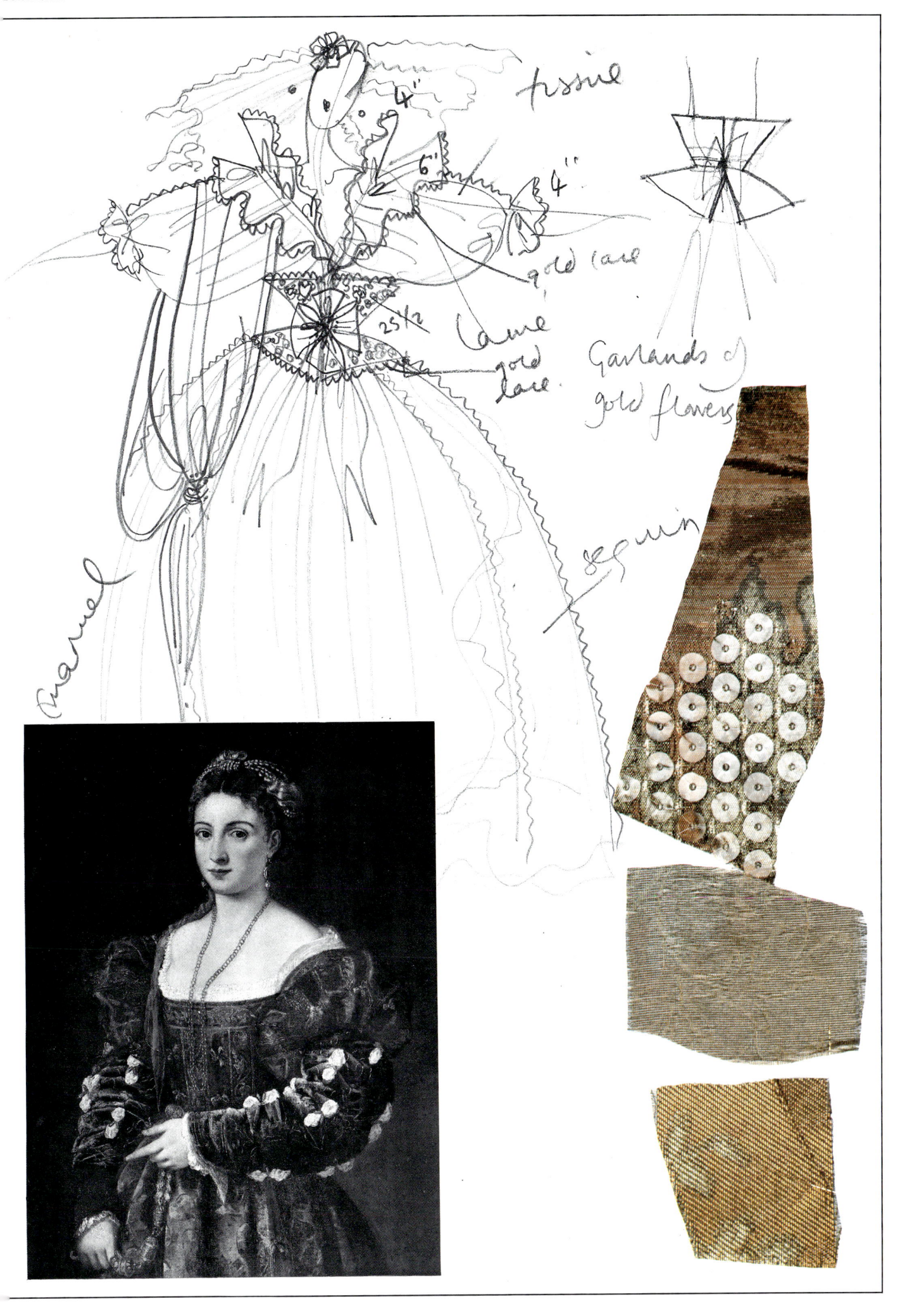

Style for all Seasons

Autumn

124   *Style for all Season*

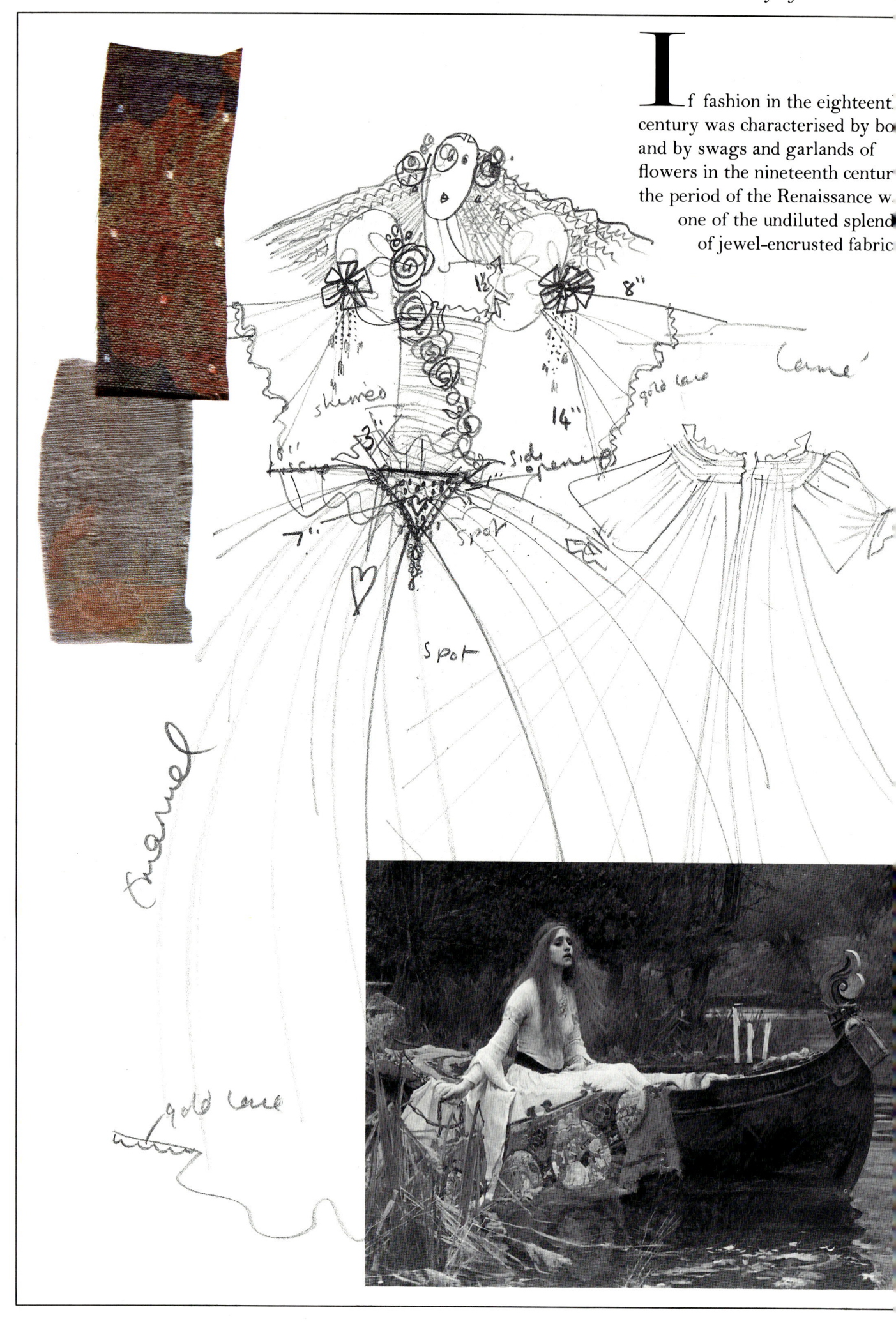

I f fashion in the eighteent
century was characterised by bo
and by swags and garlands of
flowers in the nineteenth centur
the period of the Renaissance w
one of the undiluted splend
of jewel-encrusted fabric

Autumn

Many of the dresses were so heavily jewelled and embroidered that they can almost be considered as wonderful pieces of jewellery in themselves, as you can see if you look at any portrait of Elizabeth I, the Italian Renaissance beauties or the Pre-Raphaelite revival of this mood.

Style for all Seasons

Autumn

Sophie Ward is the eighteen-year-old daughter of the actor Simon Ward, and to us, she is also the spirit of the English rose. Her classic English blonde looks can appear to be both as translucent as Spring or as mysterious and shadowy as a Pre-Raphaelite heroine of Autumn. Here, she is photographed in that complete expression of late Victorian fantasy—Leighton House, Holland Park. Built by Lord Leighton, the late-Victorian academician, the Arab hall is the *pièce de résistance* of this extraordinary house. Sophie, like any teenager, is more likely to be seen in jeans than in one of our Pre-Raphaelite dresses, but she has that intangible quality of adding something extra to anything she wears to create an illusion that that particular dress, or indeed, that pair of jeans, could never look quite so beautiful or graceful on anyone else.

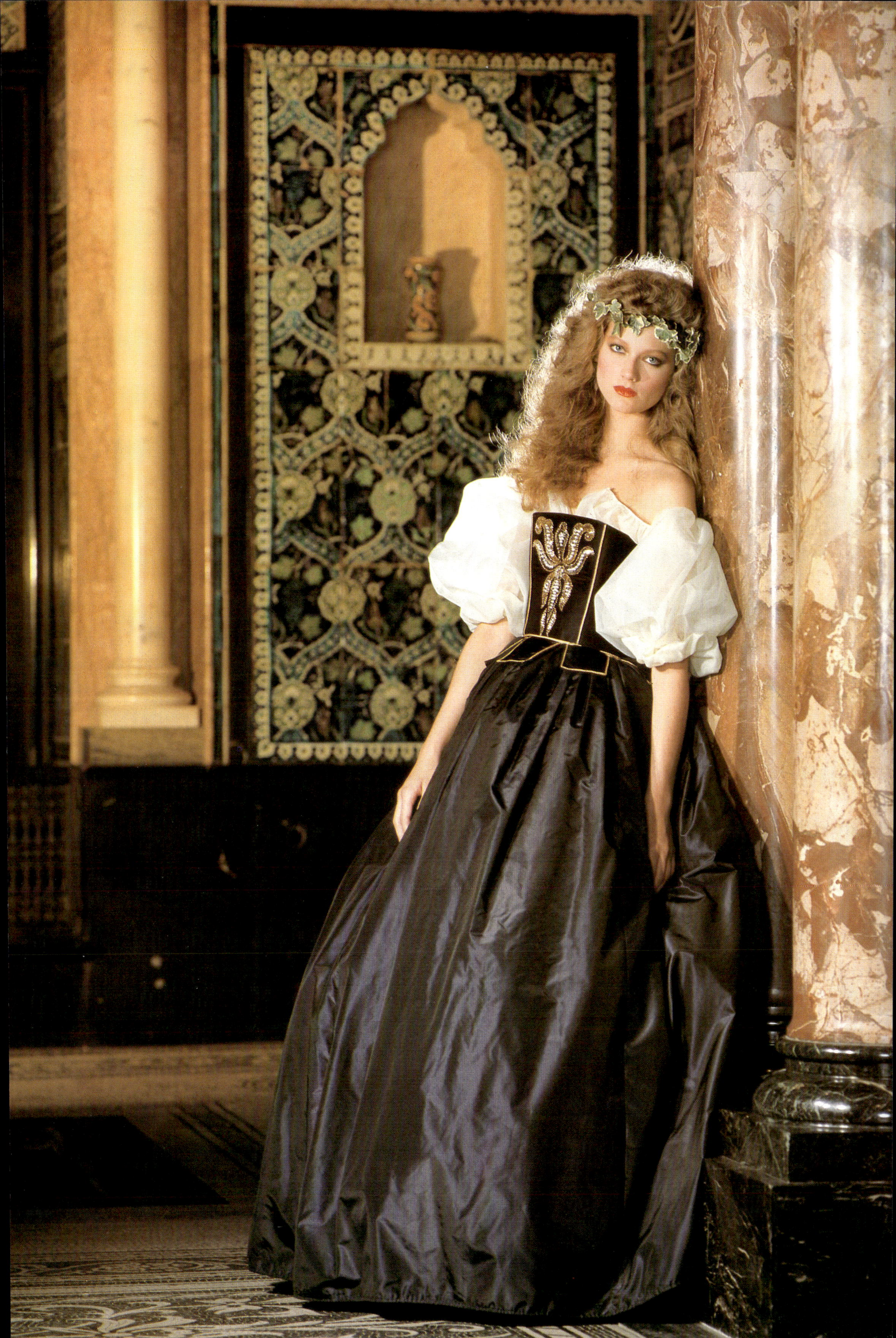

WINTER

rich deep black, arctic white...
...hollyberry red...
the icy glitter of diamonds
against the luxurious
disorder of fur

Style for all Seasons

Winter

Claire Bloom, our spirit of Winter, is one of the most distinguished actresses of her generation. From the time she starred as a new discovery in *Limelight* with Charlie Chaplin, to her present non-stop career starring as Lady Marchmain in *Brideshead Revisited*, or touring with her own one-woman recitals and readings, Claire Bloom is superb. Her pensive, delicate beauty reminded us of the dark magnificence of a Goya portrait.

'I tend to wear very simple clothes, but for recitals I love this sort of look. I love fur and I have a mink coat which I don't seem to wear very much, but I would love an extravagant red fox. These clothes really do make me feel as if I'd stepped out of a painting.'

Here she wears a dress for winter dances in black silk taffeta with a simple trellis design of jet black sequins on the bodice, which is subtly echoed by the muted sparkle of the black lacquered wreath in the background.

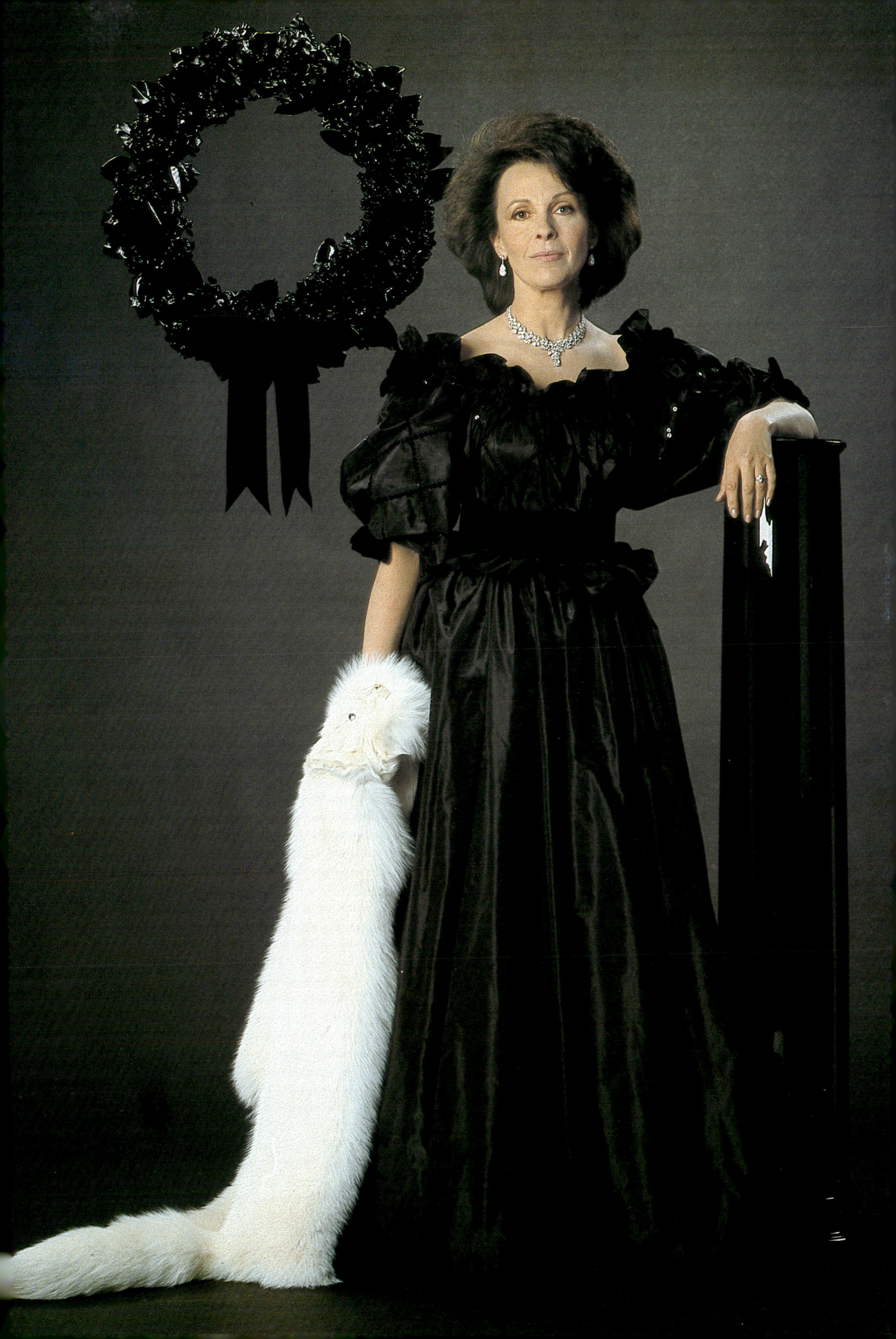

We carry ideas through to create a variety of effects on a similar theme. The richness of Winter is brought to life here in a black taffeta dress with a trellis of gold sequins overall. It is romantic in a rather different way from our summer effects—more sophisticated, more subtle, and a more mature expression of feminine beauty. Inspirations for this look come from Renaissance paintings, particularly Spanish, Venetian and Elizabethan portraits. The trellis effect was frequently used in the fifteenth century, when the embroidery was made up of rubies, pearls and other precious stones. Today, we usually buy the fabric already over-embroidered, and then perhaps add some flourishes of our own.

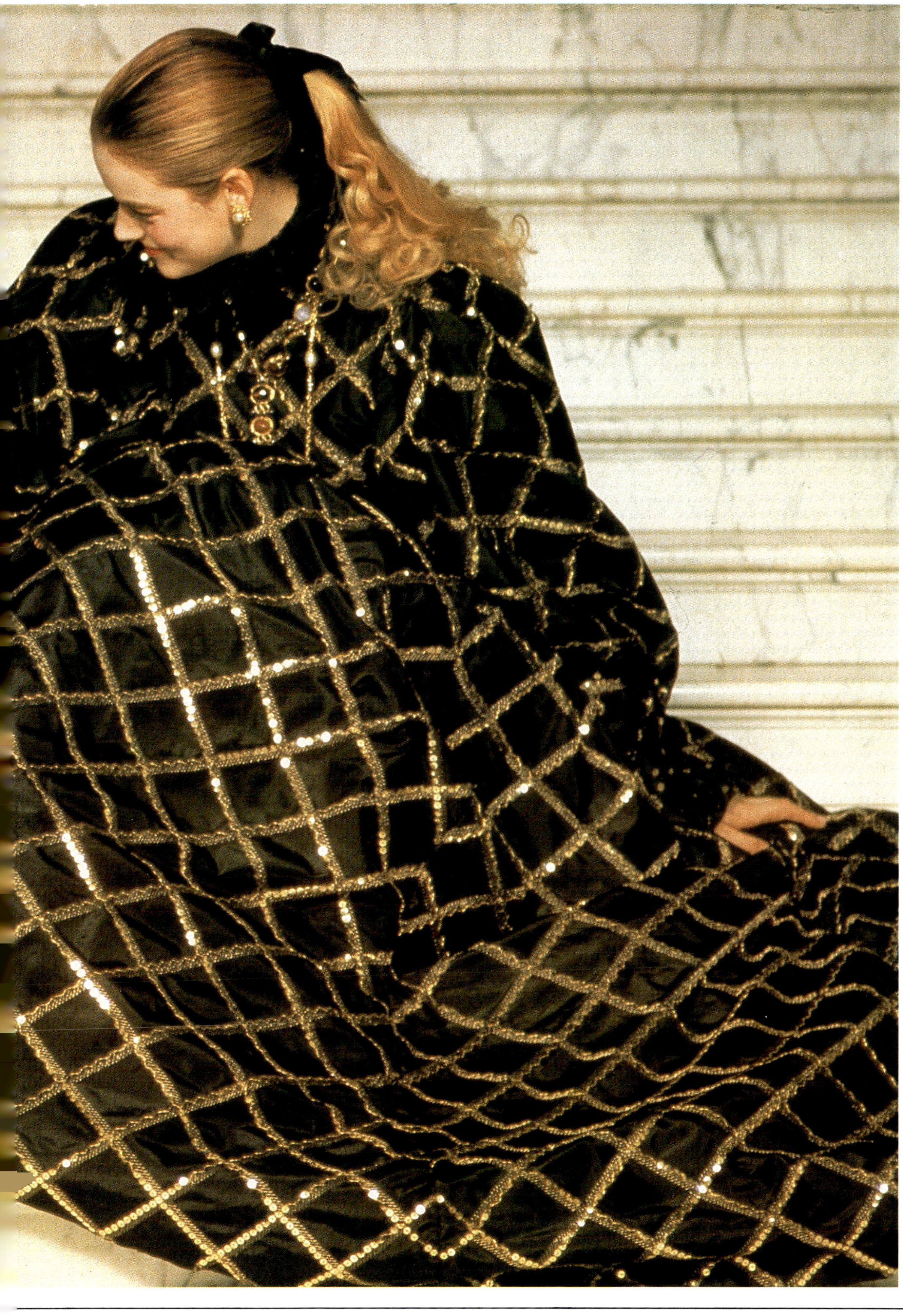

Winter demands a certain realignment of make-up to heighten colour. We liked this picture taken for a December cover of *Harpers & Queen* because the make-up is porcelain clear, but strong enough to balance the deep, glowing red and rich black of the dress.

We were asked by *Harpers* to make the dress specially for the cover and not only did it have to be finished within two days, but it had to reflect the influence of the Spanish painter Velazquez. Thanks to our seamstress we managed it, from initial sketch to finished dress, but only just. It is an interesting example of creating a dress for a specific picture, which is something we seem to do more and more. We were very aware that as the dress was to appear on the cover, as well as inside the magazine, it should have some careful detailing at the neck, to focus attention on the face.

It is a principle that is worth remembering when deciding what to wear for an occasion that demands two different views of a dress—perhaps for a special dinner, where only the bodice of the dress will be seen for a large part of the evening. Focus on the face is important for stylish entrances too—a huge dramatic cape, with stiff ruffles round the neck, and enormous flowers are two of the ways we introduce drama to winter evenings. Overleaf: The complete dress, photographed for *Harpers & Queen*, is the centrepiece in this re-creation of a baroque Spanish scene.

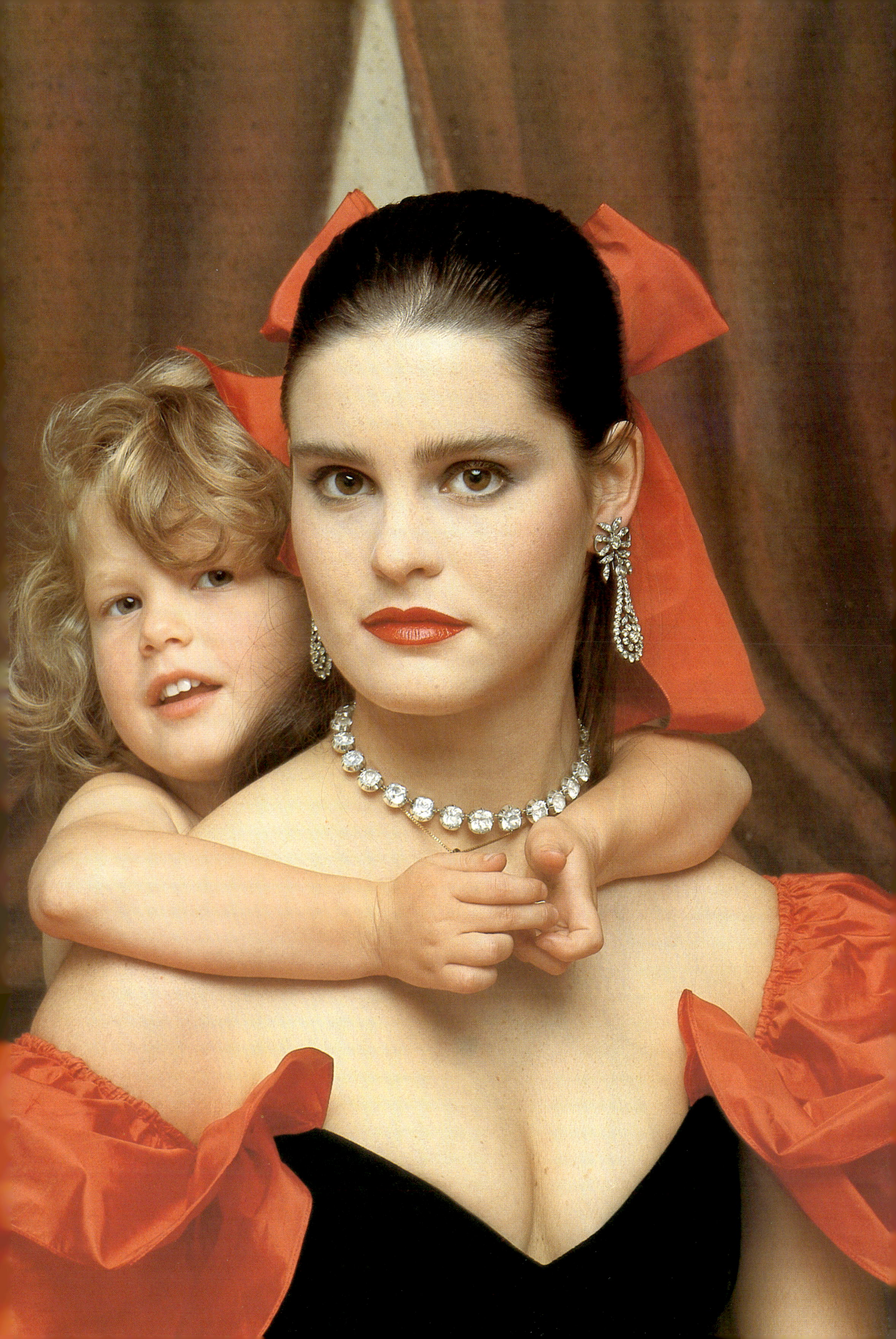

Style for all Seasons

Winter

Style for all Seasons

For some time now, a more pronounced structure has been creeping back into style. Dresses which depend on boning and cutting to give them shape and to mould the body represent a trend recently endorsed by French designers. This style is in total contrast to casual, unconstructed clothes, and we believe in it as a stunning and dramatic look for winter evenings.

We have always admired the finished effect produced by strapless ballgowns with perhaps a stiff ruffle or a matching stole to soften the effect. On the left is our design in black silk taffeta for the Princess of Wales, which she wore to a charity evening at Goldsmiths Hall—her first official engagement after the announcement of her betrothal to the Prince of Wales.

Winter 143

The American designer Charles James was a past-master of this sort of design and achieved a very definite sculptural effect as can be seen from the Cecil Beaton photograph of his ballgowns, shown above.

On the following pages are our thoughts on this rather abstract look, inspired by the new structuralism and photographed by John Swannell.

The vital point to remember about these structured, minimal dresses is that they are designed to focus attention not just on the face, but on the neck, shoulders and arms too, and a light dusting of gold-tinted powder not only creates a pretty effect, but evens up the tone of the neck and shoulders to prevent too severe a contrast with the face.

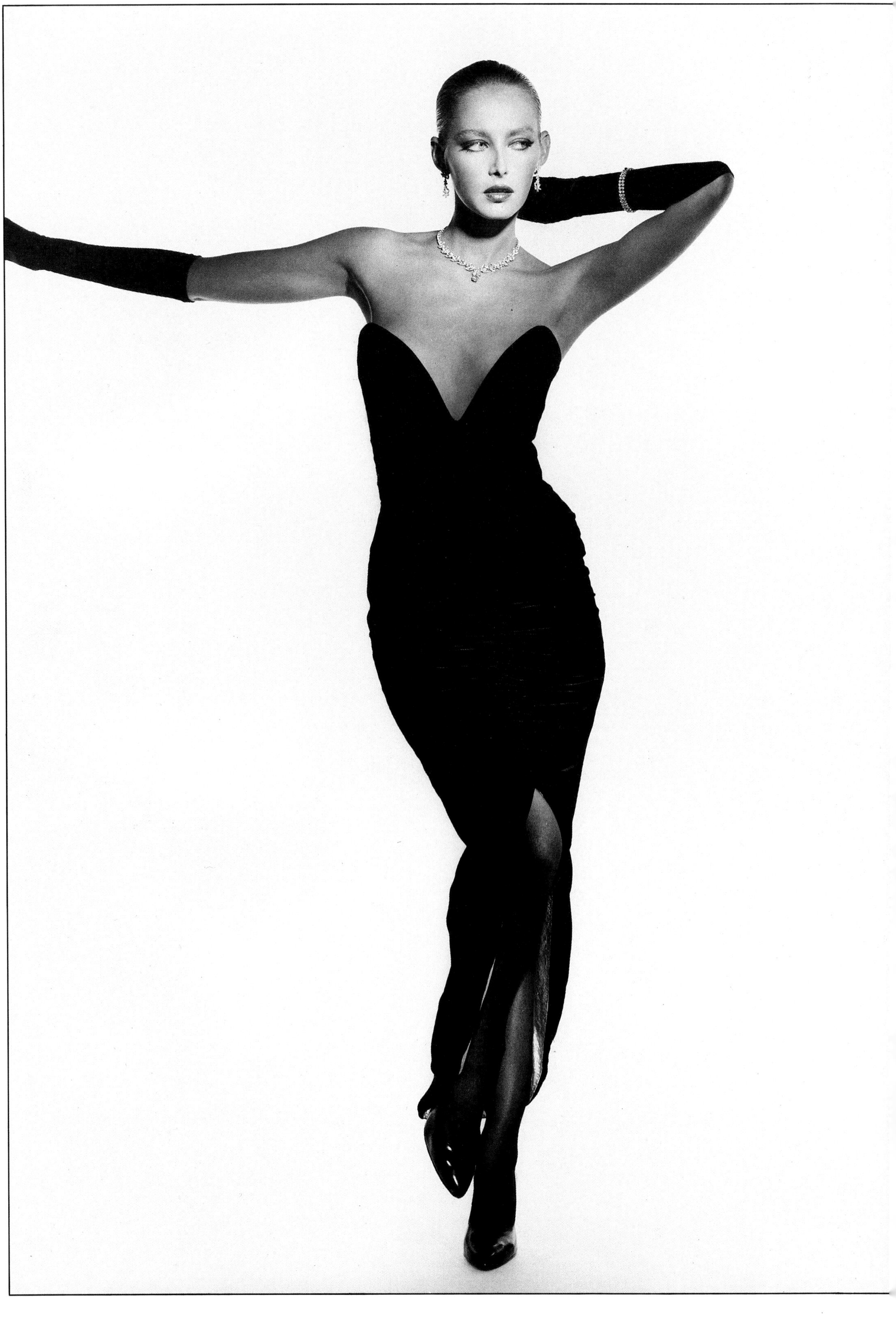

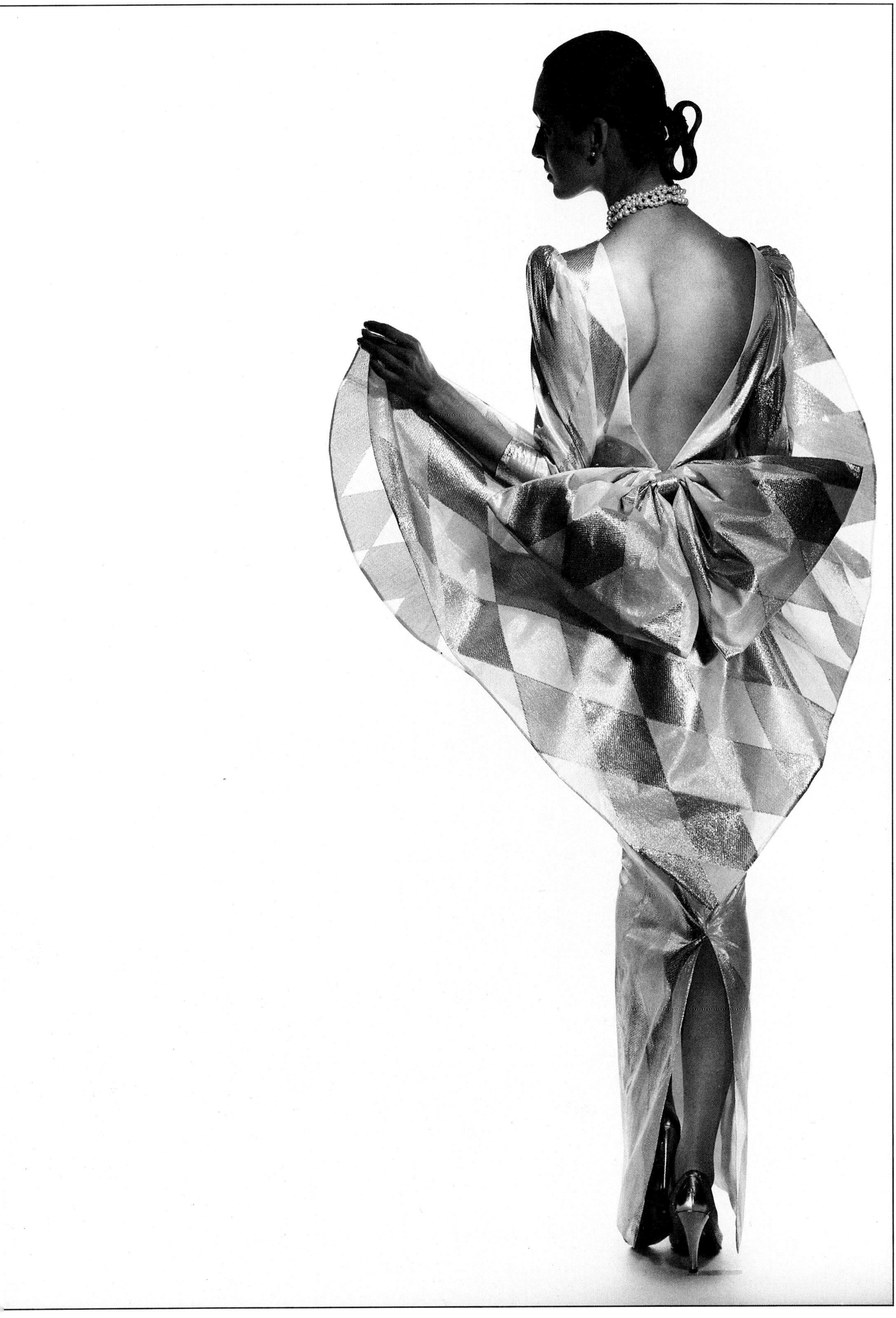

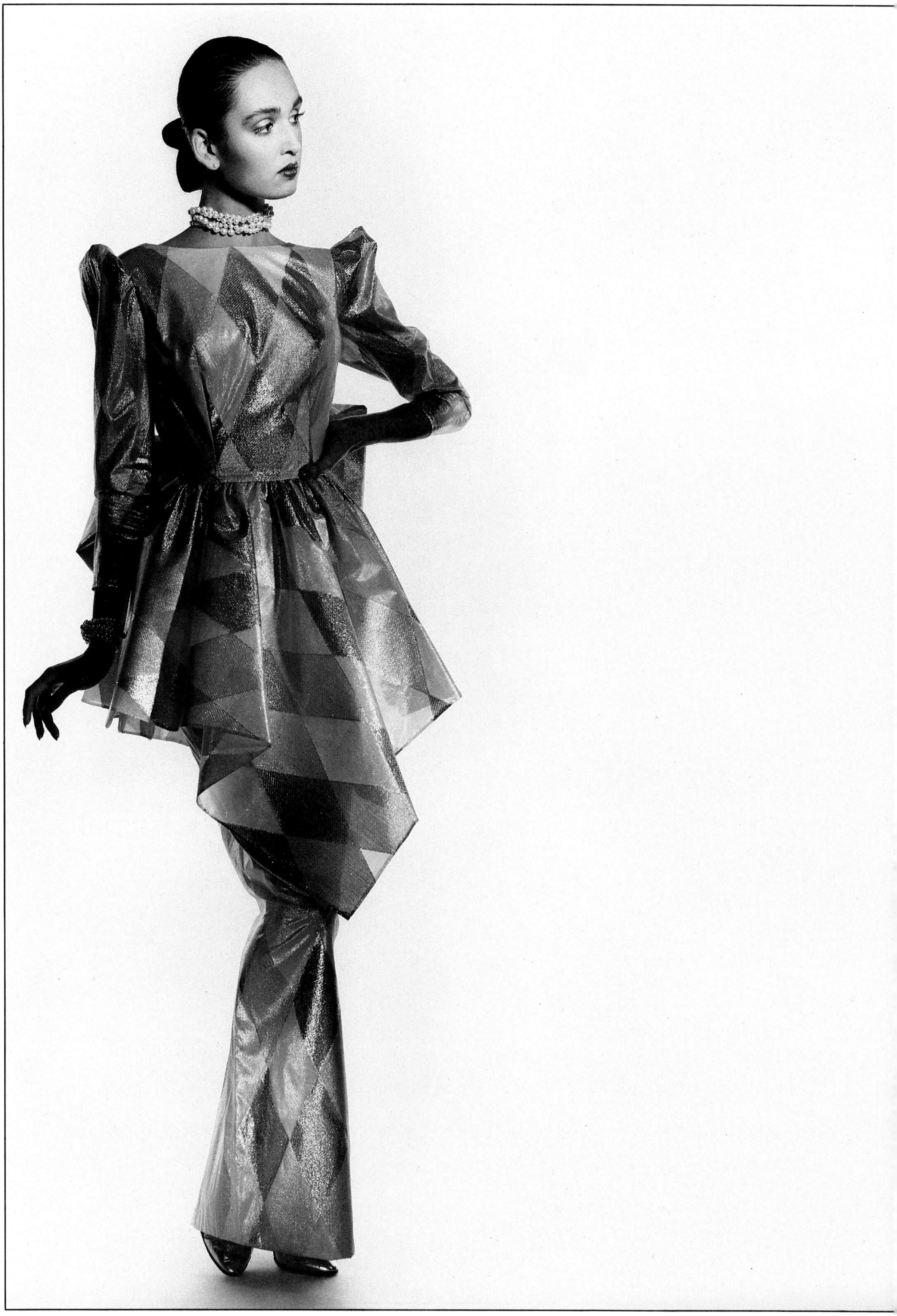

Winter

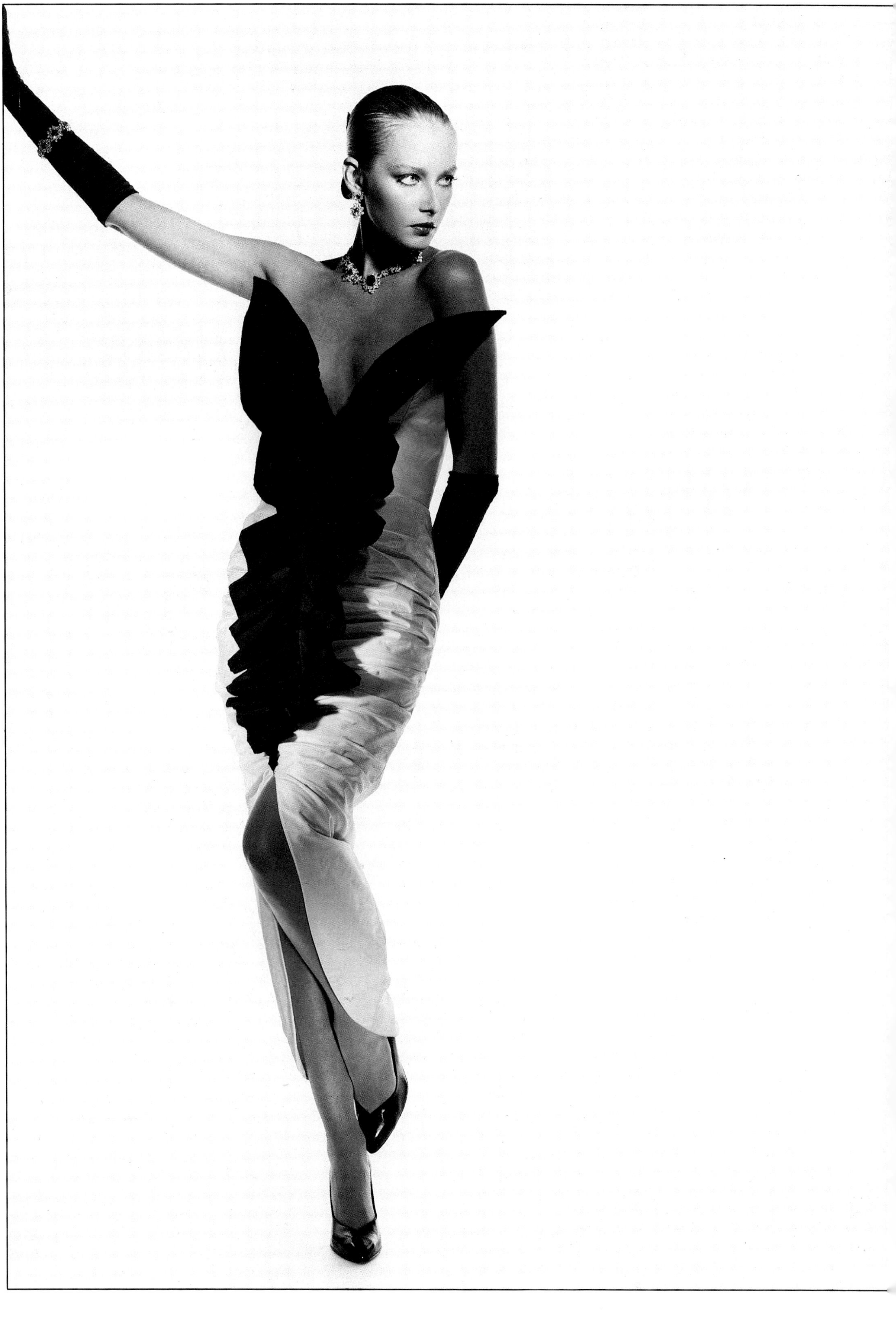

Winter

Greta Garbo has been an inspiration for all romantic seasons, because she lent to everything she wore a unique aura of self-contained glamour. Whatever she wore seemed to become almost an extension of herself, which is how we always hope our dresses will look.

We have always been inspired by Garbo in her great romantic roles in the films *Anna Karenina*, *Camille* and *As You Desire Me*. Even the exaggerated conventions of MGM's historical costume design do nothing to diminish her dignity and beauty. No matter how large the crinoline, or voluminous the ruffles, she imparts an air of cool distinction to everything she wears. Personality is the quality that makes dresses, such as these Garbo-inspired ideas we have sketched opposite, come alive – imbued with the confidence of their wearer.

Winter

W̲e also use sequins for witty little touches of fantasy, as with this 'stars and moons' dress, where we sequinned new moons onto midnight blue tulle. Winter is mystery and imagination . . . dark corners, shadows cast by firelight. And, of course, effects to match.

Winter

Another glamorous solution to winter dressing-up is simply all-over sequins. Inspired by Norman Norell (right) who in turn was inspired by the twenties couturiers such as Jean Patou, our solid sequin sheath (below) continues this classic couture tradition.

Glitter can be dramatically pretty too; we have already mentioned the sequinned wedding dress we designed for Candia Wallop, and here is another idea with the same underlying theme. Heart of ice—our frozen dreams wedding dress in white taffeta encrusted with sequins—had a frosted bouquet to complete the snow queen image.

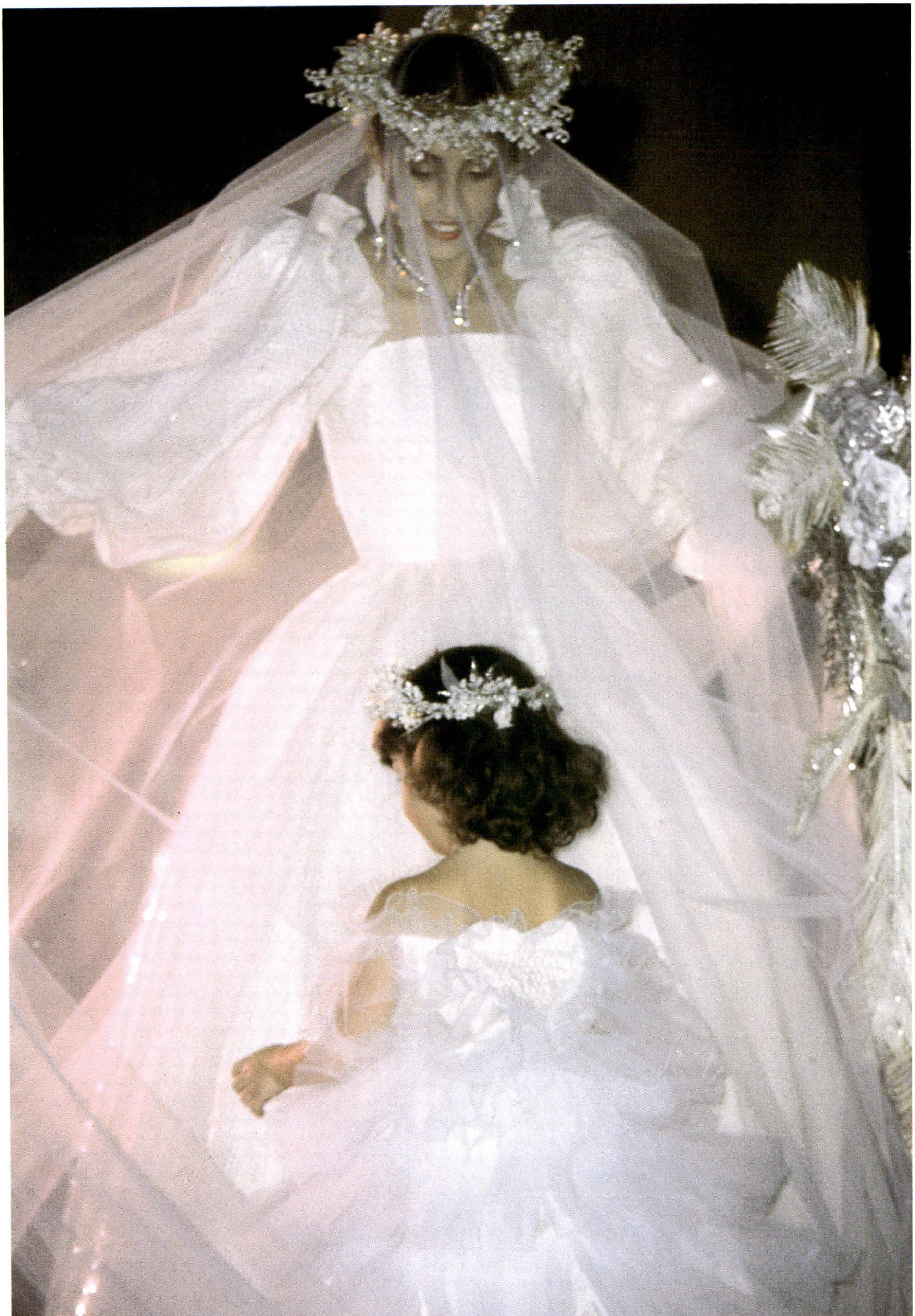

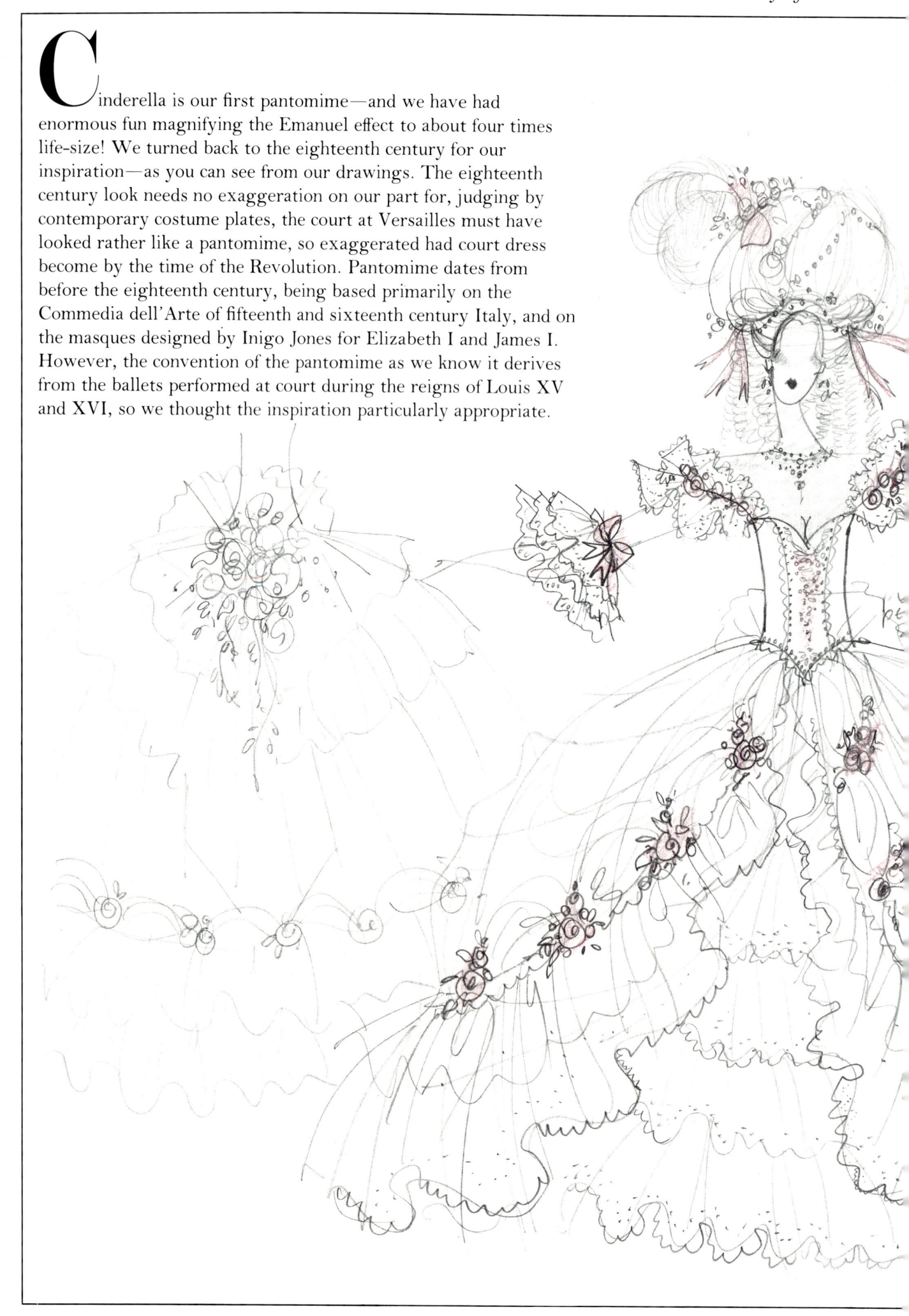

Cinderella is our first pantomime—and we have had enormous fun magnifying the Emanuel effect to about four times life-size! We turned back to the eighteenth century for our inspiration—as you can see from our drawings. The eighteenth century look needs no exaggeration on our part for, judging by contemporary costume plates, the court at Versailles must have looked rather like a pantomime, so exaggerated had court dress become by the time of the Revolution. Pantomime dates from before the eighteenth century, being based primarily on the Commedia dell'Arte of fifteenth and sixteenth century Italy, and on the masques designed by Inigo Jones for Elizabeth I and James I. However, the convention of the pantomime as we know it derives from the ballets performed at court during the reigns of Louis XV and XVI, so we thought the inspiration particularly appropriate.

Winter 157

Faye Dunaway's magnificent blonde beauty is dramatically captured in this photograph taken by her husband, Terry O'Neill, especially for this book. Since her début in *Bonnie and Clyde*, she has consistently surprised and intrigued filmgoers by her ability, rare among superstars, to transform herself utterly to meet the demands of the parts she plays, most recently by her eerie metamorphosis into Joan Crawford in *Mommie Dearest*. This dress was designed for her appearance at last year's Cannes Film Festival (see below), and yet wearing it here there are echoes of the title role she was rehearsing at the time when this photograph was taken, for Michael Winner's film of the famous tale set in Restoration England, *The Wicked Lady*.

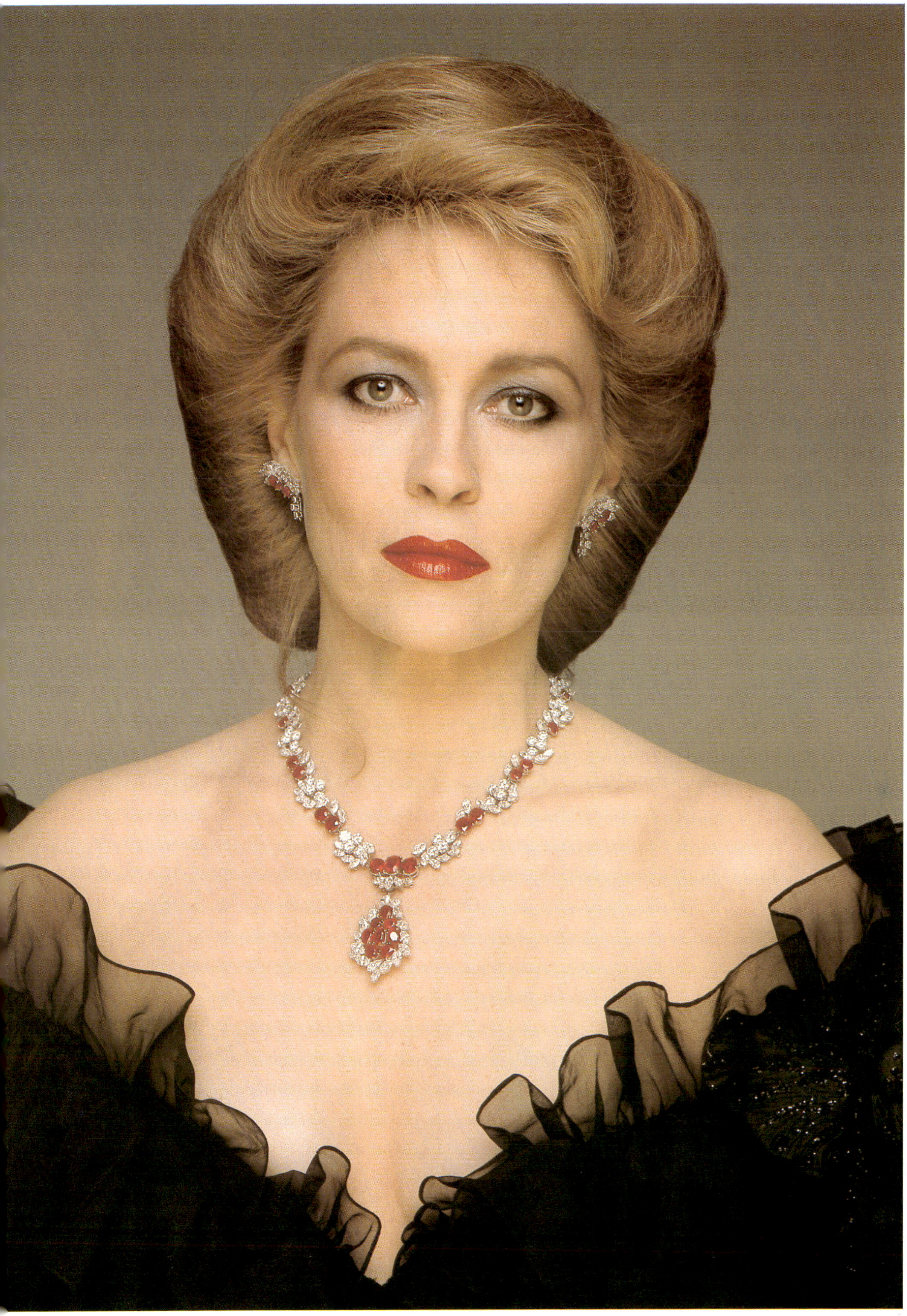

'Dressed in a dream'—a tissue of delight
A thousand beauties that can catch the flow
Of dawns and sunsets—keep perpetual, bright
Spring's golden gardens, Winter's silver snow.
Does not this bring to living what it lacks—
The sacrament that holds off mortal time
And makes life proofed against those close attacks
By choice of what remains a better clime?
'Dressed in a dream' our work makes time stand still
Continuous only in the wish you make
To choose life's favours, beauty's mandate fill
To wear what time can never now forsake.
'Dressed in a dream', a vision brought to be
From dream to fact by life's velleity!

JIM H. 26 June 1982

This poem was handed to us, quite unexpectedly, when we were photographing one of our dresses on location at a museum in London. One of the curators, seeing the dress, wrote it for us. We think it expresses so eloquently certain ideas we ourselves find difficult to put into words, that we have chosen it as the conclusion to this book.